PLAIN ENGLISH

Handbook

Ninth Edition

J. Martyn Walsh
Anna Kathleen Walsh

Random House/McCormick-Mathers

Workbooks to accompany Plain English Handbook

PLAIN ENGLISH 1
PLAIN ENGLISH 2
PLAIN ENGLISH 3
PLAIN ENGLISH 4

International Standard Book Number: 0-800-93023-1

Manufactured in the United States of America

Contents

Preface

This is a complete handbook containing all the rules, definitions, and illustrations necessary for mastery of the functional grammar and usage of English.

The treatment of grammar presented here is entirely descriptive. It is based on authoritative studies of the language as it is actually used in the United States, and not on anyone's opinion of what usage should be. Naturally, in view of the scope and purpose of this handbook, the usage presented pertains to standard written usage, except where otherwise noted. The problems of informal speech or colloquial expression are too varied and complex to be contained in a single volume. Insofar as informal discourse should be natural, it is not a subject of instruction. The levels of usage are, of course, clearly explained in this book.

The sections are numbered consecutively throughout the book to make effective cross-referencing possible. Numbers in parentheses in the text itself refer to sections in the book.

1

Sentence Completeness

Effective sentences result from applying many functional elements: good logic, good syntax and grammar, thoughtful focusing of ideas, careful variation to avoid monotony, and proper emphasis in setting forth important thoughts and images. To a large extent, effectiveness is dependent upon the proper use of modifiers. It is the sentence modifiers that qualify and particularize, giving the sentence the clarity and precision that is the mark of good writing.

The Sentence and Its Parts

1 A **sentence** is a word or a group of words that expresses and conveys a complete thought from a speaker or writer to a listener or reader. When written, it begins with a capital letter:

   The book is on the table.

2 A sentence must have a **subject** and a **predicate**, either expressed or implied (understood), and it may have an object complement or other complements, modifiers, connectives, and independent elements.

3 The **subject** is that about which something is said:

   Flowers bloom.   *Shakespeare* wrote many great plays.
   Squirrels climb trees.   *Denver* is in Colorado.

4   The **predicate** is that which is said about the subject:

Flowers *bloom.*   Shakespeare *wrote many great plays.*
Squirrels *climb trees.*   Denver *is in Colorado.*

DIAGRAM—Sentence with *simple subject* (13) and *simple predicate* (15):

Fish swim.

5   A sentence must have a subject and a predicate in order to be grammatically complete, but in an **elliptical sentence** (a sentence or clause from which a word or words are properly omitted) either the subject or the predicate or both may not be expressed:

Subject omitted: (*You*) Read this story.
Predicate omitted: Who spoke? John (*spoke*).
Subject and predicate verb omitted: What did I bring? (*I brought*) Books.

6   The receiver of the action denoted by the simple predicate (15) is the **direct object** (sometimes called the **object complement**):

The carpenter built a *house.*

The girls picked *corn.*

DIAGRAM—Sentence with *direct object* of a verb:

Farmers grow *wheat.*

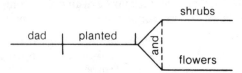

The direct object may be **compound:**

We saw *rocks* and *trees.*

DIAGRAM—Sentence with *compound direct object* of verb:

Dad planted *shrubs* and *flowers.*

7   A **modifier** is a word or a group of words that qualifies and characterizes the meaning of another word:

    She ran *quickly*. (*Quickly* modifies *ran*.)
    The tall blond man laughed. (*The, tall,* and *blond* modify *man*.)
    The boy *at the desk* is Fred. (*At the desk* modifies *boy*.)
    The girl *whom you saw* is Jane. (*Whom you saw* modifies *girl*.)

    DIAGRAM—Sentence with *modifiers* of subject and predicate:

    The concerned young woman spoke *frankly*.

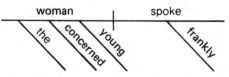

8   A group of related words not having a subject and a predicate is called a **phrase**:

    The book *on the desk* is a grammar.

9   A group of related words having a subject and a predicate and used as a part of a sentence is called a **clause**:

    Mary is the girl *who swam*. (Subject is *who*; predicate is *swam*.)

10   Although a sentence or a clause must have a subject and a predicate, either can be correct with only one word expressed:

    Go. (**sentence**)
    The coach said, "Go." (**clause**)

In both the sentence and the clause above, the omitted subject *you* is clearly understood.

11   **Connectives** (sometimes called **connectors**) serve to join the sentence parts:

    He came *with* me. (**preposition,** 44)
    Girls *and* boys play tennis. (**conjunction,** 45)

12   **Independent elements** are expressions that have no grammatical connection with the sentence in which they are found. They are of several kinds:

    1. **Interjection:** *Hurrah!* we won.
    2. **Direct address:** *Ruth,* I want you to help me.
    3. **Exclamation:** *Poor dog!* It needs our help.
    4. **Parenthetical limiting expresson:** He went, *I am sure,* to please us.
    5. **Responsive:** *No,* he has not come.
    6. **Nominative absolute:** *The work being done,* we went home.

Most independent elements are set off from the rest of the sentence by commas (500), but the interjection and the exclamation are set apart by exclamation marks (531).

13   **The simple subject** is the subject taken without any modifier (7):

A noisy *crowd* gathered immediately.

The simple subject may consist of more than one word (**compound noun,** 60):

Betty Ruth Mills is a lawyer.

The *flour mill* burned down.

14   The **complete subject** is the simple subject with all its modifiers:

The first game began early.

The girl at the pool is Evelyn.

15   The **simple predicate** is the predicate taken without any modifier or complement. The simple predicate may consist of more than one word, for it may include a main verb and its helpers (a **verb phrase,** 41):

The boy *has waited* patiently.

The book *should have been returned* to the library.

16   The **complete predicate** is the predicate with all its complements and modifiers:

The girl *ran swiftly.*

The visitor *was admiring the paintings in the entrance hall.*

17   A **compound subject** is one made up of two or more simple subjects:

Flowers and *trees* are beautiful.

18   A **compound predicate** consists of two or more simple predicates:

Children *work* and *play.*

19   Both the subject and predicate may be compound:

Girls and *boys study* and *play.*

Diagram—Sentence with *compound subject* and *compound predicate:*

Boys and *girls play* and *sing.*

Classification of Sentences

20 Sentences are classified according to their structure, or form, **as simple, compound,** and **complex.** (A less common type, the **compound-complex,** is described in section 416.)

21 A **simple sentence** has only one independent clause (397) and no dependent clause (398):

> Our team won the game.

Both the subject and predicate of a simple sentence may be compound (19):

> Mark and Ruth played and sang at the party. (A simple sentence may have any number of phrases—*at the party* is a phrase—but it can not contain a dependent clause.)

22 A **compound sentence** is equivalent to two or more simple sentences (called **independent clauses** when used in a single sentence) connected by **coordinating conjunctions** (367) or by punctuation:

> Joe studies hard, and he enjoys school.
> Joe studies hard; he enjoys school.
> Joe studies hard. He enjoys school.

Notice the three ways of writing these words. The last way is not a compound sentence; it is two simple sentences.

23 A **complex sentence** is one that contains but *one* independent clause (397) and one or more dependent clauses (398):

> I was not at home when he came. (The clause *when he came* is dependent.)

♦ Although the definition for the complex sentence given above is the conventional one, there is another type of complex sentence in which the independent clause is not at once evident. In this type a noun clause (400–407) may be an essential element of the independent clause:

> *That she is intelligent* is obvious. (**subject**)
> The truth is *that he forgot.* (**predicate nominative**)
> She said *that she would accept the offer.* (**object**)

24 As to function, sentences are divided into four classes: **declarative, imperative, interrogative,** and **exclamatory.**

25 A **declarative sentence** makes a statement or asserts a fact:

> Our glee club sings well.

26 The **imperative sentence** expresses a command, request, or entreaty:

> Do not walk on the grass. (The subject of an imperative sentence is *you*; it is usually omitted.)

27   The **interrogative sentence** asks a question:

    Where shall we go?   Whom will we meet?   What will we do?

28   The **exclamatory sentence** expresses surprise or a strong emotion:

    What a great day it's been!   **How beautiful the sunset is!**

    A declarative, an interrogative, or an imperative sentence may also become exclamatory when expressed excitedly; therefore, not all grammarians list the exclamatory sentence as a separate class.

29   The **natural** or **normal order** of the sentence is for the subject to precede the predicate:

    George went to school.

30   When the complete predicate or some part of it precedes the subject, the sentence is in **inverted order:**

    Down the shute came tons of wheat.

    In an interrogative sentence (27) and in a sentence beginning with the expletive (239) *there* or the adverbs *here* or *there*, the predicate or a part of it usually precedes the subject:

    Have you *received* the book?
    There *are* three books on the desk.
    There your book *will be found.*
    Here *comes* Rose.

31   END PUNCTUATION   Correct punctuation at the end of a sentence is very important. The declarative sentence (25) ends with a period. The imperative sentence (26) ends with a period. The interrogative sentence (27) closes with a question mark. The exclamatory sentence (28) usually ends with an exclamation mark:

    The trees are most colorful in autumn. (**declarative**)
    Come to see me next winter. (**imperative**)
    Do you like English? (**interrogative**)
    How quiet these forests are! (**exclamatory**)

32   CAPITALIZATION   Every English sentence (except one in parentheses within another sentence) begins with a capital letter. This is a very important rule.

Writing Good Sentences

33   Do not omit the subject from a declarative sentence:

    Incorrect: Saw you at the show last night.
    Correct: I saw you at the show last night.

    (Subjects are properly omitted from imperative sentences (26).)

34 **Do not write a fragment of a sentence as if it were complete:**

Incorrect: He studied hard. Hoping to learn it all. (The words *hoping to learn it all* form a phrase that modifies *he*.)

Correct: He studied hard, hoping to learn it all.

Incorrect: Anne had a good time. While she was in the East last summer. (The words *while she was in the East last summer* form a dependent clause used as an adverbial modifier.)

Correct: Anne had a good time while she was in the East last summer.

35 **Do not write two or more sentences together as one, without punctuation:**

Incorrect: We started early we were eager for the trip.

Correct: We started early. We were eager for the trip.

Correct: We started early; we were eager for the trip.

36 **Learn to distinguish a sentence from a fragment and from a group of more than one sentence.** An ability to distinguish between a sentence and a group of words that is more or less than a sentence is called **sentence sense.**

While we waited for the train. (This group of words, which resembles a dependent clause, is not a sentence; it is a fragment.)

Men and women running. (Because these words do not have a predicate, they do not form a sentence.)

They are running. (This group of words is a sentence. It expresses a complete thought and has both a subject and a predicate.)

Ask your teacher to help you. (This is an imperative sentence. The subject *you* is understood.)

Janice plays basketball she is captain of the team. (Two sentences are incorrectly written as one. This can be corrected in three ways:
1. Janice plays basketball. She is captain of the team.
2. Janice plays basketball; she is captain of the team.
3. Janice plays basketball, and she is captain of the team.)

That was a good game our boys played well were you there? (Three sentences are incorrectly joined as one. This can be corrected: That was a good game. Our boys played well. Were you there?)

37 **Do not splice sentences or independent clauses together with a comma:**

Incorrect: My brother studies French, he hopes to be a translator.
(Two sentences are incorrectly written as one.)

Correct: My brother studies French. He hopes to be a translator.

2

The Parts of Speech

A DEFINITION, formal and exact, must include all that belongs to the object defined and exclude all that does not; an EXPLANATION, general, may simply throw light upon some point of special difficulty; a DESCRIPTION, pictorial, may include only some general features. In all good writing these three concepts must always be distinguished so that the reader may readily understand the viewpoint of the writer.

Definitions

38   All words may be classified into eight groups called **parts of speech.** The group to which a word belongs is determined by its use in the sentence; therefore, the same word may be any one of several parts of speech, depending upon its use in a given sentence. The eight parts of speech are **noun, pronoun, verb, adjective, adverb, preposition, conjunction,** and **interjection.**

39   A **noun** is the name of a person, place, thing, idea, or quality.

Robert Frost wrote *poems.*   *Ann* lives in *Boston.*
Work brings *satisfaction.*   *People* like *admiration.*

40   A **pronoun** is a word used to take the place of a noun. Through its use, one may avoid repeating name words:

Mary has lost *her* book.   The box has lost *its* handle.
Ruth saw the boys and talked with *them.*

41 A **verb** is a word used to express action, being, or state of being:

José *painted* a picture.   The law still *exists*.
That woman *is* a banker.

A verb may be composed of several words, called a **verb phrase**:
This book *should have been sent* to the storeroom.

42 An **adjective** is used to modify a noun or a pronoun. An adjective may be a single word, a phrase, or a clause:

We saw *beautiful* valleys and *rugged* mountains. (**single words**)
The rug *on the floor* is blue. (**adjective phrase**)
The man *who spoke* is a teacher. (**adjective clause**)

43 An **adverb** is used to modify a verb, an adjective, or another adverb. It may be a single word, a phrase, or a clause:

He sang *beautifully*. (**single word**)
The stranger came *into the room*. (**adverbial phrase**)
Robert left *when I came*. (**adverbial clause**)

In some cases adverbs may modify other parts of speech (316).

44 A **preposition** shows the relation between its object and some other word in the sentence:

We walked *through* the woods. (*Through* shows the nature of the relation between *woods*, its object, and *walked*, the verb.)

45 A **conjunction** connects words or groups of words:

Bob *and* Linda are here.   She came *but* she did not stay.

46 An **interjection** expresses strong feeling: *Ouch! Oh!*
The interjection has no grammatical relation to the rest of the sentence.

47 A **substantive** is any word or group of words that is used as a noun (39) or as a noun equivalent (61).

48 **Inflection** is any change in the spelling or the form of a word to indicate a change in its meaning: *book—books, I—me, has—have.*

I *have* the *book* here.   He *has* the *books* for *me*.

49 The inflection of nouns and pronouns is called **declension** (144, 159): *man—men, he—him.*

He is a friendly *man*.   The *men* are with *him*.

50 The inflection of adjectives and adverbs is called **comparison** (291–295, 327): *big—bigger—biggest, fast—faster—fastest.*

The *big* boy ran *fast*, and the *bigger* boy ran *faster*, but the *biggest* boy ran *fastest* of all.

51 The correct arrangement of the inflection of verbs is called **conjugation** (see 205).

52 The use and recorded meaning of a word in a given sentence determines what part of speech it is; therefore, while a word may be one part of speech in a particular sentence, it may be used as a different part of speech in another sentence:

You must not *rock* the boat. (**verb,** 41)

We saw a *rock* fence. (**adjective,** 42)

That *rock* is beautiful. (**noun,** 39)

The word *but* may be almost any part of speech. (**noun,** 39)

We walked *but* a short distance. (**adverb,** 43)

All came *but* Ann. (**preposition,** 44)

We waited for him, *but* he did not come. (**conjunction,** 45)

They made five yards on the first *down*. (**noun,** 39)

Karen made a *down* payment on the car. (**adjective,** 42)

We walked *down* the hill. (**preposition,** 44)

The old house fell *down*. (**adverb,** 43)

Adversity will never *down* Bob. (**verb,** 41)

The following are a few examples of the great number of words that may be commonly used as two or more parts of speech: *while, right, walk, rain, cry, play, paper, water, call, ground, land, stone, after, before, fast, outside, iron, last, paint, past, picnic, round, still, that, fly.*

Your dictionary will record the various meanings that a given word has developed in the course of its history as a word and will label the part of speech of its different meanings.

Nouns

53 There are two general classes of nouns: **common** and **proper.**

54 A **common noun** is the name that refers to a class or to anyone of a class of persons, places, or things:

The *man* walked down the *street*.   The *cow* is a domestic *animal*.

55 A **proper noun** is the name of a particular person, place, or thing; it should be capitalized:

We are *Americans*.   *Jane* was born in *Alaska*.

Apollo 15, with three astronauts, was launched on July 26, 1971.

♦ Some proper nouns have become the generic or class names of things and are not capitalized.

We read about *ohms, volts,* and *amperes* in a book about electricity. (from Ohm, Volta, Ampère)

56 In addition to these general classes of nouns there are special classes: abstract, concrete, collective, compound.

♦ **The verbal noun**, though it is not in the strictest sense a pure noun, is very important. (See 61.4, 61.5, 200, 265–268.) It has some characteristics of both noun and verb, and it may in form be either an infinitive (199) or a gerund (200):

Writing business letters is important work. (*Writing* is a gerund (200) used as subject of the sentence, but it retains verb force sufficiently to have *letters* as its object.)

To write good letters requires skill. (*To write* is an infinitive (199) used as the subject of the sentence; *letters* is the object of the infinitive.)

57 An **abstract noun** is a noun that names a quality or attribute:

We like *honesty* and *courtesy.*

58 A **concrete noun** is a noun that names something in its material form:

A *telephone* is on the *desk.*

59 A **collective noun** is a noun that is singular in form but names a **group** or collection (92, 240):

Our *school* has a strong football *team.*

60 A **compound noun** is a noun made up of two or more words. Some compounds are written as separate words, some are hyphenated, and others are written as one word: *fountain pen, maple syrup; secretary-general, father-in-law; fireplace, newspaper.*

The only safe guide for determining the correct form of a compound is a dictionary.

♦ Some grammarians classify such nouns as *Duke of Wellington* and *Chase Manhattan Bank* as **phrasal nouns.**

61 **Noun equivalents** include words (other than nouns) and groups of words (phrases and clauses) that fulfill noun functions. Examples are:

1. **Pronoun** (40): *She* is my teacher.
2. **Adjective** (42): The *young* are full of energy.
3. **Adverb** (43): Since *then* I haven't seen him.
4. **Gerund** (200): *Walking* is good exercise.
5. **Infinitive** (199): *To win* is not our real intention.
6. **Phrase** (8): *Over the top* is our aim.
7. **Clause** (9, 396, 399): *That he has gone* is a fact.
8. **Quotation:** *"The time has arrived,"* the speaker said. (See 401.)

62 The **modifications** of nouns are gender, person, number, and case.

63 **Gender** is distinction as to sex; therefore, there are logically but two classes of gender. However, the following four are described by many grammarians: **masculine, feminine, neuter, common.**

64   A noun that denotes a **male** is of the **masculine gender:** *man, boy, father, brother.*

65   A noun that denotes a **female** is of the **feminine gender:** *woman, girl, mother, sister.*

66   A noun that names an object without sex is of the **neuter gender:** *book, rock, desk, house.*

67   Nouns that may denote either male or female or both are said to be of **common gender:** *student, child, singers, teachers.*

68   There are three ways of indicating gender:

    1. Change of word: *man—woman, rooster—hen.*

    2. Addition of a descriptive word: *salesman—saleswoman.*

    3. Use of a suffix: *host–hostess, hero–heroine.*

◆ There is a tendency to avoid making gender distinctions when they are not essential, for example, use *poet* rather than *poetess.*

69   **Person** denotes the speaker, the person or thing spoken to, the person or thing spoken of. There are three classes: **first, second, third.**

    Nouns used alone are always in the third person. When a noun is used in apposition to a pronoun, the pronoun determines the person of the verb.

70   The **first person** denotes the person speaking:

    I, Fred Smith, am willing to go.

71   The **second person** denotes the person or thing spoken to:

    You, Lola, are selected for the honor.

72   The **third person** denotes the person or thing spoken of:

    Our *coach* is here now; *she* will help us.

73   **Number** shows whether the noun refers to one or to more than one person, place, or thing. There are two classes: **singular, plural.**

74   **Singular number** denotes one: *tree, desk, book.*

75   **Plural number** denotes more than one: *trees, desks, books.*

Plurals of Nouns

A dictionary is the only complete guide in forming plurals.

76   Form the plurals of **most nouns** including those **ending in silent e,** by adding *s* to the singular: *bird—birds, tree—trees, tube—tubes.*

77   Form the plurals of nouns **ending in s, ss, x, z, zz, ch, tch, sh** by adding *es* to the singular: *gas—gases, guess—guesses, box—boxes, fez—fezes, buzz—buzzes, church—churches, ditch—ditches, bush—bushes.*

78   Form the plurals of most nouns **ending in o preceded by a consonant** by adding *es* to the singular: *hero—heroes, potato—potatoes.*
Some exceptions to this rule are: *piano—pianos, solo—solos.*

79   Form the plurals of nouns **ending in o preceded by a vowel** (vowels are *a, e, i, o, u,* and sometimes *w* and *y*) by adding *s* to the singular: *radio—radios, trio—trios, two—twos.*
The plurals of a few nouns **ending in o** are formed by adding either *s* or *es* to the singular, but *es* is usually preferred: *volcano—volcanoes (volcanos,) zero—zeroes (or zeros).*

80   Form the plurals of **common nouns ending in y preceded by a consonant** by changing *y* to *i* and adding *es*: *cry—cries, sky—skies.*
Form the plurals of all **proper nouns ending in y** by adding *s*:

We went to the party with the *Kellys.* Three *Henrys* and two *Marys* were there.

81   Form the plurals of nouns **ending in y preceded by a, e, o, u** by adding only *s*: *day—days, turkey—turkeys, buoy—buoys, guy—guys.*

82   Form the plurals of some nouns **ending in f or fe** by changing the *f* or *fe* to *v* and adding *es*: *sheaf—sheaves, wife—wives, half—halves.*
Other examples are *calf, elf, leaf, life, self, knife, loaf, thief, shelf.*

83   Form the plurals of other nouns **ending in f or fe** by adding only *s*: *fife—fifes, roof—roofs.*
Other examples are *belief, chief, gulf, grief, safe, strife, cliff, proof.*

84   Form the plural of some nouns **by changing vowels** within them: *goose—geese, foot—feet, man—men, woman—women.* Note: *mouse —mice.*

85   Form the plurals of these two nouns by adding *en* or *ren: ox—oxen, child—children.*

86   The plurals of **compound nouns** (60) are usually formed by adding *s* or *es* to the main word of the compound; but the plurals of some are formed by adding *s* at the end, and for others the first part of the word is pluralized; in a few cases both words are pluralized: *father-in-law—fathers-in-law, suitcase—suitcases, knight templar—knights templars* (or *knights templar*).

87   Form the plurals of nouns **ending in ful** by adding *s* at the end. Do not make the mistake of placing the *s* before the last syllable.
She used three *spoonfuls* (not *spoonsful*) of sugar.

88   Form the plurals of letters, symbols, figures, and words regarded as words by adding *'s*, or sometimes just *s*:

Dot your *i's*, cross your *t's*, and make your *3's* (or *3s*) plainer.

You have too many *and's* (or *ands*) in this sentence.

It happened in the *1890's* (or *1890s*).

89 Some nouns have the same form in both numbers: *deer, sheep, trout.*

90 Some nouns are plural in form but singular in use: *measles, mumps, ethics, news, summons.*

91 A few nouns are used in the plural only: *scissors, tongs, trousers.*

92 **Collective nouns** are singular when the group is considered a unit but plural when the individuals are indicated:

The *team* (as a unit) built *its* reputation on honesty.

The *class* (as individuals) have received *their* diplomas.

93 Some foreign words retain their original foreign plurals: *crisis—crises, axis—axes, thesis—theses, cactus—cacti, alumna—alumnae.*

94 The **case** of a noun or pronoun shows its relation to other words in the sentence. There are three cases: **nominative, possessive,** and **objective,** but nouns show case change only in the possessive form. The nominative and objective cases of nouns are used only descriptively now, but these terms help to explain grammatical terms such as *nominative absolute* and *adverbial objective.*

Uses of the Nominative Case

95 The **subject** of a finite verb, that is, one limited by number and person, is in the nominative case:

Mary wrote a book. (A *finite* verb can be used as a predicate, while the *infinite* forms—infinitive, participle, and gerund—cannot be so used.)

96 The **predicate nominative** is in the nominative case:

George is my *friend.*

It was *she.*

She was made *captain.* (289)

A noun or pronoun that completes the meaning of the predicate and denotes the same person or thing as the subject is a **predicate nominative** (sometimes called **subjective complement,** 179.3).

♦ See predicate adjective (179.4, 278, 289).

DIAGRAM—Sentence with a noun as *predicate nominative,* or *subjective complement:*

The girls were *students.*

DIAGRAM—Sentence with *compound predicate nominative* or *subjective complement*:

The trees are *cedars* and *maples*.

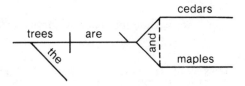

97 A **noun of direct address** is in the nominative case:

Tom, lend me your book.
Will you help me, *Tom*, with this problem?
When will we finish it, *Tom*?

♦ The noun of address is used to call the attention of the one spoken to. It is separated from the rest of the sentence by a comma or commas (500).

98 A noun of direct address is spoken with a distinctive intonation.

99 The **nominative absolute** is a substantive (47, 61) used in an absolute construction:

The rain having ceased, we went home. (499)
The night being cold, I wore an overcoat.

♦ The absolute construction is a word or a phrase related to the thought of the sentence in which it is found, but not grammatically related to any word of the sentence. It is usually made up of a noun and a participle (201, 269), either with or without modifiers (7). The absolute construction is easily changed into a clause:

The work being completed, we went home.
The work completed, we went home. (*Being* is very frequently omitted in writing.)
When the work was completed, we went home. (**clause,** 9, 396)

The absolute construction is set off from the rest of the sentence by a comma (499). Never use a period for this purpose:

Incorrect: The work being completed. We went home.
Correct: The work being completed, we went home.

100 A substantive may be in the nominative case by **apposition**:

Ms. Jones, *my teacher*, is in Chicago. (in apposition with the subject)
That is Ms. Jones, *my teacher*. (in apposition with the predicate nominative)

The substantive used in apposition—**appositive**—differs from one used in the predicate nominative (96) in that it has no verb to connect it with the word which it explains. In the two illustrations given, *my teacher* is set off by commas and no verb is used to connect *teacher* with *Ms. Jones.*

DIAGRAM—Sentence with *noun in apposition with the subject:*

Miss Smith, the *teacher*, bought a book.

101 An **appositive** is a word, a phrase (393), or a clause (404–407) placed after a substantive (47) to explain it. In 100 the word *teacher* explains who *Ms. Jones* is. The appositive is nearly always in the same case as the word which it explains (but see 118), and it is usually set off by commas (500):

> Ms. Jones, my *teacher*, writes books. (**appositive word**)
> Mr. Barnes, *driving his car*, met us at the airport. (**appositive phrase**)
> The fact *that he is coming* makes us happy. (**appositive clause**)

Although the appositive is thought of usually as a substantive (47), a modifier may be used appositively. The adjective is frequently used appositively (277), just as it is often used in the predicate (278):

> The tree, *tall* and *beautiful*, stood near the lake. (*Tall* and *beautiful* are used appositively to explain the kind of tree.)
> The tree near the lake was *tall* and *beautiful*. (*Tall* and *beautiful* are used in the predicate, 289, to describe *tree*, and the linking verb *was*, 180, is used as a connective.)

Uses of the Objective Case

102 The **direct object** of a verb is in the objective case:

> Richard painted the *picture*.

The direct object is sometimes called the **object complement** (179.1). It completes the predicate by naming the receiver of the action in the active voice (184).

103 The direct object of a verb is also said to be in the **accusative case**, but this term is now infrequently used in English terminology.

104 The **predicate objective**, or **objective complement** (179.2), may follow verbs of *making, naming, calling, choosing, appointing, considering,* and *thinking,* and would appear in the position after the direct object; the second object completes the meaning of the predicate and relates to the direct object.

We elected Laura *captain*.

We thought her a good *leader*.

105 The **indirect object** is in the objective case:

Mary gave *Alice* a book.

The **indirect object** may be changed into a prepositional phrase, which then follows the direct object:

Mary gave a book to *Alice*.

The preposition (44) used in forming such a phrase is either *to* or *for*.

DIAGRAM—Sentence with *indirect object*:

His mother gave the *boys* some cookies.

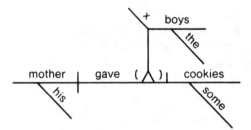

106 The **object of a preposition** is in the objective case:

The great plane flew over the *house*. (object of *over*)

107 The **adverbial objective** is a noun (with its modifiers) used as an adverb:

The child walked *three miles*.   The water was *ankle deep*.

The **adverbial noun** is joined to a verb, an adverb, or an adjective to express time, distance, measure, weight, or value. It may be modified by an adjective, such as *three* in the first example.

108 The **subject of an infinitive** (199, 272) is in the objective case:

James believed the *teacher* to be his friend.

There is no need for the *students* to help.

109 The **complement** of the infinitive *to be* having a subject is in the objective case:

James believed the teacher to be his *friend*.

John thought her to be *me*. (272)

When the infinitive *to be* has no subject, the complement is in the nominative case:

Ann wishes to be the *villain* in the play.
He was thought to be *I*. (273)

110 The **direct object of an infinitive** is in the objective case:

Helen likes to paint *pictures*.   The judge tried to help *him*.

111 A substantive may be in the objective case by **apposition** (100, 101):

We admire Dr. Brown, our *physician*.
We heard from Mrs. Hill, our *principal*.

112 The **object of a participle** (201, 269) is in the objective case:

Waving his *hand*, the boy rode away.

113 The **object of a gerund** (200, 266) is in the objective case:

Playing *games* is fun.

114 The **cognate object** is in the objective case:

She ran a good *race*.

When the object of a verb expresses an idea similar to that of the verb itself, the object is called **cognate**:

He sleeps a peaceful *sleep*.   He fought a good *fight*.

115 The **retained object** is in the objective case:

I was given a *watch* by my father.

A retained object is one that has been retained after a verb has been changed from active (184) to passive (185) voice:

My father gave (active) me a *watch*. (direct object)
I was given (passive) a *watch* by my father. (retained object)
A watch was given *me* by my father. (retained object)

Note that either the direct or indirect object may be retained.

Uses of the Possessive Case

116 The **possessive case** denotes ownership, possession, or a similar relationship:

This is *Robert's* book.

♦ The possessive case is referred to as the **genitive case** by some grammarians.

117 The noun (or pronoun, 146) in the possessive case is used as a modifier, and as a modifier it is sometimes called a **possessive adjective** (131, 146, 281):

He found *Sylvia's book*. (*Sylvia's* modifies *book*.)
The *girl's* hair is brown. (*Girl's* modifies *hair*.)

118 A noun in the possessive case may be used as an appositive of another noun (100, 101):

> Bob drives his brother *Harry's* car.

Notice that *brother* would have the possessive form (his *brother's* car) if the appositive were omitted.

119 Ownership or possession may be denoted by the noun in a phrase introduced by *of*:

> the *poems of Keats*   the *music of Schubert*

This is the form most widely used with inanimate things:

> The *leaves of the tree* (instead of the *tree's leaves*) are falling.

But many neuter nouns (66) are correctly used with the regular possessive form, although there is no ownership involved. Here are a few of these: *a week's work, a dime's worth, for pity's sake, heart's desire, yesterday's report, time's flight.*

Possessive Forms of Nouns

120 To form the possessive singular of a noun, use an apostrophe and *s* after the word (519): the *boy's* cap, the *girl's* book.

It is correct to use either the apostrophe alone or *'s* in forming the possessive singular of a proper noun ending in *s*:

> Did you see *Phyllis'* new car?   She carried *Chris's* book.

Form the possessive of a noun of two or more syllables ending in *s* or an *s*-sound and not accented on the last syllable by adding the apostrophe only:

> He did it for his conscience' sake.

121 Form the possessive of a plural noun that ends in *s* by adding the apostrophe only:

> The two *boys'* caps are torn.

> The three *students'* books are here.

122 To form the possessive of a plural noun not ending in *s*, add an apostrophe and *s*:

> *men's* shoes, *oxen's* horns

123 In forming the possessive of a compound, place the possessive ending after the last word: *Queen of England's throne, sister-in-law's farm.*

The possessives of plurals of compounds (86) are formed in the same way:

> *brothers-in-law's* farms

124 When two nouns are used to indicate common ownership, the sign
of possession is placed after the second noun:

Smith and Brown's office (Smith and Brown occupy the same office.)

125 When two nouns are used to show separate ownership, add the sign
of possession to both nouns:

Opal's and Edna's coats are the same color.

126 In such phrases as *nobody else,* the possessive is formed by placing
the sign at the end of the phrase:

nobody else's business

127 The noun or pronoun introducing a gerund (200) is its subject. The
subject of a gerund is usually in the possessive case:

She told us of *Jane's* winning the prize.

He asked me about *my* writing the story.

Pronouns

128 A **pronoun** is a word that substitutes for a noun and that can be used
in the same position in the sentence. The classes of pronouns include
the following: **personal, relative, interrogative, demonstrative** (138,
281), **indefinite** (139, 281), **possessive** (131). The last three are sometimes called **pronominal adjectives** (131, 140, 281) because they are
used as adjectives when the substantive (47) is expressed.

129 The **antecedent** of a pronoun is the word for which the pronoun
stands:

Mary brought her book. (*Mary* is the antecedent of *her.*)

The *person* who came here has gone. (The antecedent of *who* is *person.*)

130 A pronoun generally agrees with its antecedent in **gender, person,** and
number. Its case is determined by its use in a particular group of
words. Form modifications of the pronoun are the same as those of
the noun: **gender, person, number,** and **case.**

131 An **absolute possessive pronoun** represents the possessor and the
thing possessed. It does not modify a noun directly. The absolute possessive pronouns are *mine, yours, his, hers, its, theirs, ours.*

This book is *mine.* (The word *mine* here is equivalent to *my book;*
therefore it represents both the possessor and the thing possessed.)

Some authorities classify as **possessive adjectives** (146) the forms
my, your, his, her, its, our, their, when they are used as modifiers. However, these remain pronouns and agree with their antecedents in
gender, person, and number, even when they modify nouns.

132 **Personal pronouns** show by their form whether they are the first, second, or third person (69–72). The simple personal pronouns include *I, you, he, she, it, we, they,* and their inflected forms (144).

133 **Compound personal pronouns** are formed by adding *-self* or *-selves* to some of the simple personal pronouns: *myself, yourself, himself, herself, itself, ourselves, themselves.* (*Hisself* and *theirselves* are incorrect forms.)

134 A compound personal pronoun is used correctly as a **reflexive pronoun** to refer an action to the subject of a sentence:

He helped himself.

It is also correctly used as an **intensive pronoun** in apposition for emphasis:

He himself is wrong.

A compound personal pronoun should not be used to take the place of a simple personal pronoun:

John and I (not *myself*) went to the show.

135 A **relative pronoun** is not only a pronoun but also a connecting word. It refers to a substantive (47) in the main, or independent, clause (396, 397) in which it is found, and it joins an adjective clause (408) to its antecedent. The relative pronoun has a use in the dependent clause (160, 398), such as subject, object of verb, or object of preposition, and it joins the dependent clause to an independent, or main, clause. Because the relative pronoun connects a subordinate clause with a main clause, it is called also a **conjunctive pronoun.** Words used as relative pronouns are *who, whom, whose, which, that,* and *what* (*what* has no antecedent and is equivalent to *that which*):

The boy *who* sang is here.   *What* was said is well known.

136 The **compound relative pronoun** is formed by adding *-ever* or *-soever* to certain simple relatives. The case of a relative pronoun depends on its use in its own clause:

We invite *whoever* will come.   (*Whoever* is the subject of *will come.*)

137 The **interrogative pronouns** are *who, whom, whose, which,* and *what,* when they are used in asking questions:

Who is the speaker?

138 The **demonstrative** or **adjective pronouns** (128, 139, 140, 290) point out particular persons, places, or things:

This is my pencil.   *That* is your book.

♦ The most commonly used demonstratives are *this, that, these,* and *those.* When one of these words modifies a substantive (47), it ceases to be a pronoun and becomes an adjective (140, 275, 281, 290):

That is a beautiful tree. (**pronoun**)   That tree is beautiful. (**adjective**)

139 **Indefinite pronouns** point out persons, places, or things less specifically than demonstratives do (138):

All did their work.   Many were absent today.

♦ Some of the commonly used indefinites are *everybody, everyone, anybody, nobody, each, either, neither, one, none, some, other, another, few, all, many, several,* and *both*. When one of these words modifies a substantive (47), it ceases to be a pronoun (128) and becomes an adjective (140, 275, 281, 290):

Many attended the lecture today. (**pronoun**)

Many students attended the lecture today. (**adjective**)

Some do not like this story. (**pronoun**)

Some students do not like this story. (**adjective**)

140 Words that are sometimes used as adjectives and sometimes as pronouns are often called **pronominal adjectives,** or **adjective pronouns** (128, 138, 139, 281):

Several people did their duty.   Several did their duty.

141 In using relative pronouns (135), *who* is generally used to refer to persons; *which,* to animals and things; and *that,* to either persons, animals, places, or things:

It was a woman *who* helped us.

The dog, *which* is a faithful animal, is loved by the family.

He spoke of the sailors and the ships *that* were lost.

♦ With clauses that are nonrestrictive, or defining, *who* or *which* is used; but with clauses that are restrictive, or limiting,, *that* is used by careful writers.

142 Make the pronoun agree with its antecedent (129) in number (73):

Each boy should study *his* (not *their*) lesson. (*Boy* is singular and calls for a singular pronoun.)

Case: Forms and Use of Pronouns

143 The case forms of pronouns are always determined by their own use in a sentence, never by the use of their antecedent.

Was it he *whom* they saw? (*Whom* is the object of *saw*.)

144 The nominative case forms of the personal pronouns are *I, we, he, she, they;* the objective case forms are *me, us, him, her, them*. The forms *it* and *you* are used in both the nominative and objective case. *Her* may be either objective or possessive.

Declension of Personal Pronouns

| | SINGULAR | | PLURAL | | |
	Nomina-tive	Possessive	Objec-tive	Nomina-tive	Possessive	Objec-tive
1ST PER.	I	my, mine	me	we	our, ours	us
2ND PER.	you	your, yours	you	you	your, yours	you
3RD PER.	he	his	him	they	their, theirs	them
	she	her, hers	her	they	their, theirs	them
	it	its	it	they	their, theirs	them

145 Personal pronouns (132) in the nominative case have the same uses as nouns (95–101), as follows:

1. **Subject of a verb:** *I* went home.
2. **Predicate nominative:** I am *he.*
3. **Direct address:** *You*, Fred, can give a demonstration.
4. **Nominative absolute:** *He* being ill, we did not go.
5. **Appositive:** We, Mary and *I*, played ball.
6. **Complement of the infinitive** *to be* **not having a subject:** John was thought to be *I.* (See 109, 274.)

146 Personal pronouns (132) in the possessive case **do not require the sign of possession** as do nouns. The possessive forms (see 131, 144) are *my, mine, our, ours, his, her, hers, their, theirs, its, your, yours:*

That book is *yours.* (not *your's*)

The only correct use of the apostrophe with the personal pronoun is in contractions which are often found in reported speech, but less frequently in formal written text.

It's time to go home.   They're ready to see you.

The following pronouns in the possessive case are sometimes called **possessive adjectives:** *my, your, his, her, its, our, their.* (131, 281)

147 Personal pronouns in the **objective case** (144) may be used in these ways:

1. **Direct object of a verb:** The teacher praised *her.*
2. **Indirect object:** He gave *her* a copy of the essay.
3. **Object of a preposition:** I spoke to *him.*
4. **Subject of an infinitive:** He asked *me* to stay.
5. **Complement of the infinitive** *to be* **having a subject:** Did you think Sally to be *her?* (109, 273)
6. **Object of a participle:** Seeing *me* at the door, my aunt smiled happily.
7. **Object of an infinitive:** Mary tried to help *me.* (110)

8. **Object of a gerund:** Helping *him* was my duty. (113, 200, 266)

9. **Appositive:** Ann invited us, Bill and *me*.

148 A noun or pronoun following *than* or *as* is in the nominative or objective case according to its construction in the elliptical (5) clause to which it refers:

You are stronger than *he* (is strong).

Tony is not as strong as *she* (is strong).

Carla likes him as well as *I* (do).

Carla likes him as well as (she likes) *me*.

149 When a subject or a predicate nominative is compound (17, 96), both parts should be in the nominative case form:

John and *he* are going.

The winners are Bill and *she*.

150 Do not repeat a subject by using a pronoun after it:

Charles (not *Charles he*) studied hard.

151 When a pronoun is used as the subject or as a predicate nominative and has a noun in apposition (100, 101) following it, the nominative form (144) of the pronoun should be used:

All *we* students went to the play.

It was *we* girls who did the work.

152 A personal pronoun used as a **predicate nominative** should be in nominative case form (144, 180):

The guests were *she* (not *her*) and *they* (not *them*).

♦ Some authorities feel that "It is *me*" is natural and acceptable in conversation, but careful writers prefer "It is *I*" in formal written work.

153 If a pronoun appears in the **compound object** of a **verb**, a **preposition**, or an **infinitive**, the pronoun should be in the objective case form:

Our uncle saw Clyde and *me*.   The woman spoke to Grace and *me*.

Aunt Joan hopes to see Jim and *me* tomorrow.

154 When the **indirect object** (105) is compound, all pronoun parts should be in the objective case form:

The farmer gave *her* and *me* some apples.

155 When a pronoun is the direct (147.1) or the indirect (147.2) object of a verb and has a noun in apposition (101), use the objective form of the pronoun:

Our teacher saw *us* girls.   Bob sent *us* boys a message.

156 *But*, when used in the sense of *except*, is a preposition (341) and must, like *except* and *between*, have an object:

I invited all the girls but *her*.   He stood between you and *me*.

157 When a pronoun is the object of a preposition (147.3) or an infinitive and has with it a noun in apposition (101), use the objective form of the pronoun:

Sue came with *us* students.   He came to help *us* cadets.

158 *Who, whom, whose, which,* and *what* are **interrogative pronouns** when they are used in asking questions.

159 *Who,* whether interrogative or relative, is the nominative case form:

Who did Wilma say was the speaker? (*Who* is the subject of *was;* the clause *who was the speaker* is the object of *say.*)

Whom is the objective case form:

Whom will you send to town?

I met the girl of *whom* you spoke. (**relative**)

Declension of Relative Pronouns

	SINGULAR AND PLURAL	
Nominative	Possessive	Objective
who	whose	whom
which	whose	which

160 The case form of the pronoun used as a relative (135) depends upon the use of the relative in the clause (9) it introduces:

This is the boy *who* lost his book. (*Who* is subject of *lost.*)

The man *whom* you saw is my friend. (*Whom* is object of *saw.*)

161 The compound relative *whoever* is the nominative case form:

Stop *whoever* comes this way. (*Whoever* is the subject of *comes.* The clause *whoever comes this way* is the object of *stop.*)

162 The compound relative *whomever* is the objective case form:

Send it to *whomever* you choose. (*Whomever* is the object of *choose.* The clause *whomever you choose* is the object of the preposition *to.*)

Whomever you ask will go with us. (*Whomever* is the object of *ask.* The clause *whomever you ask* is the subject of the verb *will go.*)

♦ The case forms of the compound relative *whoever* seem more easily confused than the forms of *who.* When the compound relatives are used, the form may be determined more readily if words are supplied to show an antecedent. In 161, for example, the sentence would be expanded to *You stop him who comes this way.* The example in this section would be *He whom you ask will go with us.*

Number

163 The **indefinite pronouns** *each, either, neither, one, everyone, anyone, someone, no one, anybody, somebody, everybody* are singular (242):

Each girl should do *her* best.   Neither boy could sing *his* song.

Sometimes the meaning is so clearly plural that a singular personal pronoun cannot be used to refer to the indefinite pronoun:

Everyone was so busy writing a version of the story that *they* did not notice who had come in. (Not *he* did not notice.)

♦Current informal usage permits use of the plural with various indefinite pronouns.

164 A pronoun must be singular when it refers to a noun modified by such indefinite adjectives (139, 140) as *each, every,* and *neither:*

Each boy brought *his* ticket.   Every girl brought *her* books.

165 A pronoun that refers to a collective noun (59) is singular if the group acts as a unit:

The band has won fame because of *its* leader.

But the pronoun is plural if the individuals of the group act as individuals:

The band have ordered *their* new instruments.

Usage

166 Most experts agree that *which* should not be used to refer to a complete statement (376):

Questionable: He had to work, *which* caused him to be late.
Better: He was late *because* he had to work.

167 The word *same* should not be used as a pronoun instead of *it* or *them:*

I have read your offer (offers) and have decided to accept *it* (*them*) (not *same* or *the same*).

168 *Them* is never used as an adjective nor as the subject of a sentence:

Those (not *Them* or *Them there*) books are mine.

169 *They* should not be used with indefinite reference:

People (not *They*) say that he is talented.

Verbs

170 A verb (41) is a word that expresses action, being, or state of being. A verb may be formed by a group of words; such a group is called a verb phrase, or a phrasal verb (181, 391). According to the way in which they form their principal parts (202), verbs are divided into two classes: **regular** (weak) and **irregular** (strong).

171 A **regular** (weak) **verb** forms its past tense (193) and past participle

(201) by adding *d* or *ed* to the present tense (191): *race—raced—
raced, help—helped—helped.*

172 An **irregular** (strong) **verb** usually forms its past tense and past participle by changing a vowel of the present (or infinitive, 199) form:
begin—began—begun.

Sometimes a different word may be used for a principal part: *go—
went—gone.*

Sometimes the past tense and past participle are the same: *buy,—
bought— bought;* sometimes all the principal parts are the same: *set—
set—set.*

Transitive and Intransitive

173 According to use, verbs are classified as **transitive** or **intransitive**.

174 A **transitive verb** has a receiver of the action expressed in the meaning
of the verb to complete the meaning. When the actor is the subject
(3), the receiver of the action is the object (6):

Bob *wrote* a letter.

When the receiver of the action is the subject, the verb is in the
passive voice (185) but remains transitive:

A letter *was written* by Bob.

The verb *was written* is in the passive voice. When the subject is the
receiver of the action, the name of the actor may not be expressed:

Many letters *were written.*

175 An **intransitive verb** does not require a receiver of the action expressed
in the meaning of the verb:

The eagle *flew* over the mountain.

176 Many verbs may be used as transitive in one sentence and as intransitive in another sentence:

She sings well. (**intransitive**)   She sings beautiful songs. (**transitive**)

177 Intransitive verbs are of two classes: **complete** and **linking**.

178 A **complete verb** is an intransitive verb which makes a meaningful
statement without the help of any other word:

Birds *fly*.   Fish *swim*.   The horse *drinks*.   Children *play*.

179 A verb sometimes requires a substantive (47) or an adjective (42,
275) to complete its meaning. The substantive or adjective added is
called a **complement**. There are several classes of complements:

1. **Direct object** (102), or object complement:

Bob caught the *ball*.   Carmen won the *trophy*.

2. **Predicate objective** (104), or objective complement:

They elected her *captain*.   We appointed him *leader*.

3. **Predicate nominative** (96), or subjective complement:

Browning was a great *poet.*   The woman became a *writer.*

4. **Predicate adjective** (289). The predicate adjective completes the predicate of the sentence and modifies, describes, or points out the subject of the sentence:

The roses are *beautiful.* (The predicate adjective *beautiful* completes the linking verb *are* and describes the subject *roses.*) (180)

The apple looks *good.* (289)

DIAGRAM—Sentence with *predicate adjective:*

The old woman was very *active.*

180   A **linking verb,** sometimes called a **copulative verb,** is an intransitive verb that connects the subject with a predicate substantive (47) or a predicate adjective (289). The substantive or adjective following the linking verb either means the same as the subject or describes, limits, or points out the subject:

Webster *was* a statesman.   The rose *is* beautiful.

The most commonly used linking verb is *be* in its various forms such as *am, is, was, were.* Some other verbs used as linking verbs are *seem, become, appear, prove, look, remain, feel, taste, smell, sound, turn, grow, stay, continue.*

A noun or pronoun joined to a subject by a linking verb is in the nominative case (96, 145.2, 152):

It is *he.*   That was *she.*

Auxiliary Verbs

181   An auxiliary verb is a verb that aids or helps another verb express various shades of meaning. A verb with its helper or helpers is a **verb phrase** (41, 391). Some verbs used as auxiliaries are *do* (*did*), *be* (*am, is, are, was, were*), *have* (*has, had*), *may* (*might*), *can* (*could*), *must, will, shall* (*would, should*). Some of these verbs serve not only as auxiliaries but also as main verbs:

Jack *did* bring his book. (**auxiliary**)

Jack *did* good work. (**main verb**)

182   Although the linking verb *be* (180) does not take an object, all the forms of this verb may become auxiliaries in transitive verb phrases (174):

It *is* she. (**linking**)

Ruth *is* writing a letter. (*Is* is an **auxiliary** used in forming the verb phrase *is writing; write* is a transitive verb with the object *letter*.)

The forms of *be* are used also as auxiliaries in forming the passive voice (185).

The house *was* destroyed by fire.

The report *has been* received.

183 The modifications of a verb indicate its **voice, mood, tense, person,** and **number.**

Voice

184 The **voice** of a verb indicates whether the subject of the verb acts or is acted upon. **Active voice** denotes that the subject of the verb is the actor:

The man *called* the dog.

185 **Passive voice** denotes that the subject receives the action:

The dog *was called* by the man.

The passive is always a verb phrase (41, 181, 391) composed of a form of the auxiliary (181, 208) *be* followed by a past participle (201, 208):

The letter *has been written* by the manager.

♦ Passive verbs sometimes have two receivers of the action: the subject and the retained object (115):

She was given a *scholarship*.

Mood

186 **Mood** (or **mode**) indicates the manner in which the action is conceived.

187 The **indicative mood** makes a statement of fact or asks a question:

He *is* my friend.   *Is* she a teacher?

188 The **imperative mood** gives a command or makes a request:

Shut the door.

Will you please *return* the book. (Note that a question mark is not used.)

189 The **subjunctive mood** expresses a doubt, a wish, a prayer, or a condition contrary to fact:

I wonder if it *be* true.   Peace *be* with you!

I wish I *were* a lawyer.   If I *were* you, I should go.

The **present subjunctive** occurs after verbs like *demand* (259):
I insist that he *go.*

Tense

190 **Tense** denotes the time of the action indicated by a verb. The time is not always the same as that indicated by the name of the tense.

191 The **present tense** may express action which is going on at the present time or which occurs always, repeatedly, or habitually:
  The boys *are* ready to leave now.
  They *go* by bus to school.
  She *eats* cereal for breakfast.

  The present tense may express future time:
  The train *leaves* in five minutes.

  It may be used as an historical present, referring to an event completed in past time.
  The detective *solves* the mystery just in time.

192 The **present perfect tense** expresses action completed at the present time or continuing into the present:
  He *has written* a letter to his uncle. (**completed**)
  I *have lived* here for many years. (**continuing**)

193 The **past tense** expresses action completed at a definite time in the past:
  He *wrote* the letter yesterday.

  Do not use the emphatic past tense (213) for the present perfect:
  Joe *has* (not *did*) not come yet.

194 The **past perfect tense** expresses action completed before a stated or known time in the past:
  He *had written* the letter before I saw him.

195 The **future tense** expresses action that will take place in the future:
  He *will write* the letter tomorrow.

196 The **future perfect tense** expresses action that will be completed before a stated or known time in the future:
  He *will have written* the letter before we arrive tomorrow.

197 A verb as a rule agrees with its subject in person (69–72) and number (73–75). Failure to observe this rule causes many errors:
  He *doesn't* (not *don't*) know what to do.
  Those girls *are* (not *is*) talented acrobats and gymnasts.
  ♦ See 236–249, 262.

The Verbals

198 There are three forms of the verb, called **verbals,** that are also used as other parts of speech: **infinitive, gerund,** and **participle.**

199 The **infinitive** (265) is the form of the verb usually preceded by *to* (see 232)—a function word used to indicate that the following word is an infinitive.

We like *to play* basketball.

The **present infinitive** is the same as the simple present tense form of the verb, usually preceded by *to*: *to see, to go, to do.*

The **perfect infinitive** is formed by placing *to have* before the past participle (201): *to have seen, to have gone, to have done.*

200 The **gerund** (56, 266–268) is a **verbal noun** (56) ending in *ing*. The gerund may, like any verb, take an object and it may be modified by an adjective or an adverb. A gerund is sometimes referred to as a **participial noun,** as in reality it is a participle used as a noun. The gerund is the name of an action:

Trying is commendable. (*Trying* is the subject of the sentence.)

Don enjoys *reading* history. (*Reading* is the object of the verb *enjoys* and it has its own object *history.*)

Walking rapidly is good exercise. (The adverb *rapidly* modifies the gerund *walking.*)

201 A **participle** is a verbal (198) which has some of the properties of a verb and some of the properties of an adjective. It is used, as an adjective, to modify a noun or a pronoun; it may, as a verb, take an object:

The person *waving* the flag is Robert. (*Waving* modifies *person* as an adjective and takes an object *flag* as a verb.)

The **present participle** ends in *ing* and generally describes an action going on at the same time as some other action, but it sometimes refers to time preceding that of the verb used as predicate:

Sitting here, we see the parade.

Standing at the window, I saw the parade.

The present participle is used in progressive forms of the active voice (209).

The **past participle** generally indicates completed action.

The past participle of a regular verb (171) usually has the same form as the past tense (193), but the form of the past participle of the irregular verbs (172) show numerous changes in form (204).

The terms *suggested* by the committee were fair.

This was a work *done* for others.

The past participle form is always combined with *have, has,* and *had* to form the perfect tenses (192, 194, 196).

The **perfect participle** is formed of *having* and the past particple:

Having finished the work, the people went home.

Principal Parts

202 The principal parts of a verb are the first person (70) singular (74) of the present (191) indicative (187), the first person singular of the past (193) indicative, and the past participle (201):

I go—I *went*—I have *gone.*   I *see*—I *saw*—I have *seen.*

203 Do not confuse the principal parts of irregular verbs (172):

I *saw* (not *seen*) him yesterday.

204 PRINCIPAL PARTS OF THE IRREGULAR VERBS

The reference list that follows presents the variations in form that speakers and writers of English today will need to recognize; included in the list are some verbs of quite limited present use, but they have been included for their recognition as irregular forms. Whenever more than one form is shown, the first is the more commonly used. The numbered notes will indicate special uses or limitations in use; they are keyed to the list for reference.

PRESENT TENSE	PAST TENSE	PAST PARTICIPLE
abide	abode, abided	abode
—	—	accursed,[2] accurst
arise	arose	arisen
awake	awoke	awoke
be (am, is)	was, were	been
bear (*bring forth*)	bore	born [3]
bear (*carry*)	bore	borne
beat	beat	beaten, beat
beget	begot	begotten
begin	began	begun
behold	beheld	beheld, beholden [1]
bend	bent	bent
bereave	bereaved, bereft	bereaved,[1] bereft
beseech	besought, beseeched	besought
bespeak	bespoke	bespoken
bet	bet, betted	bet
bid (*command*)	bade	bidden
bid (*money*)	bid	bid
bind	bound	bound, bounden [1]
bite	bit	bitten, bit
bleed	bled	bled
blend	blended, blent	blended, blent

PRESENT TENSE	PAST TENSE	PAST PARTICIPLE
bless	blessed, blest	blest, blessed [2]
blow	blew	blown
break	broke	broken
breed	bred	bred
bring	brought	brought
build	built, builded [4]	built, builded
burn	burned, burnt	burned, burnt
burst	burst	burst
buy	bought	bought
cast	cast	cast
catch	caught	caught
chide	chided, chid	chided, chid, chidden
choose	chose	chosen
cleave (*split*)	cleft, cleaved, clove	cleft, cleaved, cloven [1]
cleave (*adhere*)	cleaved, clove, clave [4]	cleaved
cling	clung	clung
clothe	clothed, clad	clothed, clad
come	came	come
cost	cost	cost
creep	crept	crept
crow	crowed, crew	crowed
curse	cursed, curst	cursed, curst, cursed [2]
cut	cut	cut
deal	dealt	dealt
dig	dug	dug
dip	dipped	dipped
dive	dived, dove	dived
do	did	done
draw	drew	drawn
dream	dreamed, dreamt	dreamed, dreamt
dress	dressed	dressed, drest [4]
drink	drank	drunk, drunken [1]
drive	drove	driven
drop	dropped	dropped
dwell	dwelt, dwelled	dwelt, dwelled
eat	ate	eaten
engrave	fell	fallen
feed	fed	fed
feel	felt	felt
fight	fought	fought
find	found	found
flee	fled	fled
fling	flung	flung
fly	flew	flown
forbear	forbore	forborne
forbid	forbade, forbad	forbidden, forbid

PRESENT TENSE	PAST TENSE	PAST PARTICIPLE
forget	forgot	forgotten, forgot
forsake	forsook	forsaken
freeze	froze	frozen
freight	freighted	freighted, fraught [1]
get	got	got, gotten [6]
gild	gilded	gilded
gird	girded, girt	girded, girt
give	gave	given
go	went	gone
grave	graved	graven, graved
grind	ground	ground
grow	grew	grown
hang (*suspend*)	hung, hanged	hung
hang (*execute*)	hanged, hung	hanged
have	had	had
hear	heard	heard
heave	heaved, hove [7]	heaved, hove
hew	hewed	hewed, hewn
hide	hid	hidden, hid
hit	hit	hit
hold	held	held
hurt	hurt	hurt
keep	kept	kept
kneel	knelt	knelt
knit	knitted, knit	knitted, knit
know	knew	known
lade [4]	laded	laded, laden
lay	laid	laid
lead	led	led
lean	leaned, leant	leaned, leant
leap	leaped, leapt	leaped, leapt
learn	learned, learnt [8]	learned, learnt, learned [2]
leave	left	left
lend	lent	lent
let	let	let
lie (*position*)	lay	lain
lie (*tell a falsehood*)	lied	lied
light (*set fire to*)	lighted, lit	lighted, lit
light (*descend*)	lighted, lit	lighted, lit
lose	lost	lost, lorn [4]
make	made	made
mean	meant	meant
meet	met	met
melt	melted	melted, molten [1]
mow	mowed	mowed, mown

PRESENT TENSE	PAST TENSE	PAST PARTICIPLE
owe	owed, ought [4]	owed
—	ought [5]	own [5]
pay	paid	paid
pen (*confine*)	penned	penned, pent [1]
plead	pleaded, pled, plead	pleaded, pled, plead
prove	proved	proved, proven [1]
put	put	put
quit	quit, quitted	quit, quitted
read	read	read
rend	rent	rent
rid	rid, ridded	rid, ridded
ride	rode	ridden
ring	rang	rung
rise	rose	risen
roast	roasted	roasted, roast [1]
run	ran	run
saw	sawed	sawed, sawn
say	said	said
see	saw	seen
seek	sought	sought
seethe	seethed, sod [4]	seethed, sodden,[1] sod [4]
sell	sold	sold
send	sent	sent
sew	sewed	sewn, sewed
shake	shook	shaken
shape	shaped	shaped, shapen [1]
shave	shaved	shaved, shaven [1]
shear	sheared, shore	sheared, shorn
shine	shone	shone
shoe	shod	shod
shoot	shot	shot
show	showed	shown, showed
shred	shredded, shred	shredded, shred
shrink	shrank, shrunk	shrunk, shrunken [1]
shrive	shrove, shrived	shriven, shrived
shut	shut	shut
sing	sang, sung	sung
sink	sank, sunk	sunk, sunken [1]
sit	sat	sat
slay	slew	slain
sleep	slept	slept
sling	slung	slung
slink	slunk	slunk
slit	slit	slit

PRESENT TENSE	PAST TENSE	PAST PARTICIPLE
smell	smelled, smelt	smelled, smelt
smite	smote	smitten
sow	sowed	sown, sowed
speak	spoke	spoken
speed	sped, speeded	sped, speeded
spell	spelled, spelt	spelled, spelt
spill	spilled, spilt	spilled, spilt
spin	spun, span [4]	spun
spit	spit, spat	spit, spat
split	split	split
spoil	spoiled, spoilt	spoiled, spoilt
spread	spread	spread
spring	sprang	sprung
stand	stood	stood
stave	staved, stove	staved, stove
stay	stayed, staid [4]	stayed, staid [4]
steal	stole	stolen
sting	stung	stung
stick	stuck	stuck
stink	stank, stunk	stunk
strew	strewed	strewn, strewed
stride	strode	stridden
strike	struck	struck, stricken [1]
string	strung	strung
strive	strove	striven
swear	swore	sworn
sweat	sweat, sweated	sweat, sweated
sweep	swept	swept
swell	swelled	swelled, swollen
swim	swam	swum
swing	swung	swung
take	took	taken
teach	taught	taught
tear	tore	torn
tell	told	told
think	thought	thought
thrive	throve, thrived	thrived, thriven
throw	threw	thrown
thrust	thrust	thrust
toss	tossed, tost	tossed, tost
tread	trod	trodden, trod
wake	woke, waked	woke, waked, woken
wash	washed	washed, washen [4]
wax (grow)	waxed	waxed
wear	wore	worn

PRESENT TENSE	PAST TENSE	PAST PARTICIPLE
weave	wove, weaved	woven, weaved
wed	wedded, wed	wedded, wed
weep	wept	wept
wet	wet, wetted	wet, wetted
win	won	won
wind (*twist*)	wound	wound
wind (*sound*)	winded, wound	winded, wound
(won) [4] (*accustomed*)	—	wont,[1] wonted [1]
wont [4] (*need to*)	wont, wonted	—
work	worked, wrought	worked, wrought
wring	wrung	wrung
write	wrote	written
writhe	writhed	writhed, writhen [4]

[1] The following participles are now used only as adjectives: I am *beholden* to you; the *bereaved* father; his *bounden* duty; a *cloven* foot; a *drunken* driver; *fraught* with danger; now used only in for*lorn*; *molten* gold; *pent*-up anger; *roast* beef; ill-*shapen*; a clean *shaven* face; a *sodden* meadow; a *sunken* garden; *wont* to act with spirit (rare); in his *wonted* style (rare).

[2] Used as in [1] above, but notice the shift in word stress in their pronunciation as adjectives: *accurséd, blesséd, curséd, learnéd.*

[3] Now used only in phrases such as: *born* into this world; *born* in bondage.

[4] Obsolete or archaic and no longer in use: *clave, lade, ought* (as the past tense of *owe*); *washen; writhen; won* and *wont* (as the present tense); *sod.*

[5] *Ought* is an old past form of *owe*, replaced now by *owed; ought* is now used in a present sense, you *ought* to do it. *Own* is now used as an adjective, his *own* book.

[6] *Got* is the regular past form, with *got* or *gotten* as the past participle in standard English. In formal writing, *got* is preferred in the meaning of *possess* or *have*. In spoken English, *got* and *gotten* are equally used in the sense of *acquire* or *become.*

[7] Said principally of ships; the vessel *hove* in sight.

[8] A number of verbs show two past forms, one in *-ed*, the other in *-t*, as in *learned, learnt.* In writing, the *-ed* form is preferred, while in speaking the *-t* form is very widely heard.

Conjugation

205 The **conjugation** of a verb is the orderly arrangement of its forms through its voices (184–185), moods (186–189), tenses (190–196), persons (69–72, 197), and numbers (73–75, 197).

206 CONJUGATION OF THE VERB *BE*

INDICATIVE MOOD		*Singular*	*Plural*
Present Tense		1. I am	1. we are
		2. you are	2. you are
		3. he is	3. they are
Past Tense		1. I was	1. we were
		2. you were	2. you were
		3. he was	3. they were
Future Tense		1. I shall be	1. we shall be
		2. you will be	2. you will be
		3. he will be	3. they will be
Present Perfect Tense		1. I have been	1. we have been
		2. you have been	2. you have been
		3. he has been	3. they have been
Past Perfect Tense		1. I had been	1. we had been
		2. you had been	2. you had been
		3. he had been	3. they had been
Future Perfect Tense		1. I shall have been	1. we shall have been
		2. you will have been	2. you will have been
		3. he will have been	3. they will have been

SUBJUNCTIVE MOOD			
Present Tense		1. I be	1. we be
		2. you be	2. you be
		3. he be	3. they be
Past Tense		1. I were	1. we were
		2. you were	2. you were
		3. he were	3. they were
Present Perfect Tense		1. I have been	1. we have been
		2. you have been	2. you have been
		3. he have been	3. they have been
Past Perfect Tense		1. I had been	1. we had been
		2. you had been	2. you had been
		3. he had been	3. they had been

IMPERATIVE MOOD			
Present Tense		be	be

	Present	*Past*	*Perfect*
INFINITIVES	to be		to have been
PARTICIPLES	being	been	having been
GERUNDS	being		having been

207 Conjugation of the Verb SEE

Active Voice

INDICATIVE MOOD	*Singular*	*Plural*

Present Tense
- 1. I see — 1. we see
- 2. you see — 2. you see
- 3. he sees — 3. they see

Past Tense
- 1. I saw — 1. we saw
- 2. you saw — 2. you saw
- 3. he saw — 3. they saw

Future Tense
- 1. I shall see — 1. we shall see
- 2. you will see — 2. you will see
- 3. he will see — 3. they will see

Present Perfect Tense
- 1. I have seen — 1. we have seen
- 2. you have seen — 2. you have seen
- 3. he has seen — 3. they have seen

Past Perfect Tense
- 1. I had seen — 1. we had seen
- 2. you had seen — 2. you had seen
- 3. he had seen — 3. they had seen

Future Perfect Tense
- 1. I shall have seen — 1. we shall have seen
- 2. you will have seen — 2. you will have seen
- 3. he will have seen — 3. they will have seen

SUBJUNCTIVE MOOD

Present Tense
- 1. I see — 1. we see
- 2. you see — 2. you see
- 3. he see — 3. they see

Past Tense
- 1. I saw — 1. we saw
- 2. you saw — 2. you saw
- 3. he saw — 3. they saw

Present Perfect Tense
- 1. I have seen — 1. we have seen
- 2. you have seen — 2. you have seen
- 3. he have seen — 3. they have seen

Past Perfect Tense
- 1. I had seen — 1. we had seen
- 2. you had seen — 2. you had seen
- 3. he had seen — 3. they had seen

IMPERATIVE MOOD

see   see

Present Tense	*Present*	*Past*	*Perfect*
INFINITIVES	to see		to have seen
PARTICIPLES	seeing	seen	having seen
GERUNDS	seeing		having seen

208 CONJUGATION OF THE VERB *SEE*
Passive Voice

INDICATIVE MOOD	*Singular*	*Plural*
Present Tense	1. I am seen	1. we are seen
	2. you are seen	2. you are seen
	3. he is seen	3. they are seen
Past Tense	1. I was seen	1. we were seen
	2. you were seen	2. you were seen
	3. he was seen	3. they were seen
Future Tense	1. I shall be seen	1. we shall be seen
	2. you will be seen	2. you will be seen
	3. he will be seen	3. they will be seen
Present Perfect Tense	1. I have been seen	1. we have been seen
	2. you have been seen	2. you have been seen
	3. he has been seen	3. they have been seen
Past Perfect Tense	1. I had been seen	1. we had been seen
	2. you had been seen	2. you had been seen
	3. he had been seen	3. they had been seen
Future Perfect Tense	1. I shall have been seen	1. we shall have been seen
	2. you will have been seen	2. you will have been seen
	3. he will have been seen	3. they will have been seen

SUBJUNCTIVE MOOD		
Present Tense	1. I be seen	1. we be seen
	2. you be seen	2. you be seen
	3. he be seen	3. they be seen
Past Tense	1. I were seen	1. we were seen
	2. you were seen	2. you were seen
	3. he were seen	3. they were seen
Present Perfect Tense	1. I have been seen	1. we have been seen
	2. you have been seen	2. you have been seen
	3. he have been seen	3. they have been seen
Past Perfect Tense	1. I had been seen	1. we had been seen
	2. you had been seen	2. you had been seen
	3. he had been seen	3. they had been seen

IMPERATIVE MOOD		
Present Tense	be seen	be seen

	Present	Past	Perfect
INFINITIVES	to be seen		to have been seen
PARTICIPLES	being seen	seen	having been seen
GERUNDS	being seen		having been seen

209 Conjugation of the Verb *SEE* — Progressive Form

Active Voice

INDICATIVE MOOD	*Singular*	*Plural*
Present Tense	1. I am seeing	1. we are seeing
	2. you are seeing	2. you are seeing
	3. he is seeing	3. they are seeing
Past Tense	1. I was seeing	1. we were seeing
	2. you were seeing	2. you were seeing
	3. he was seeing	3. they were seeing
Future Tense	1. I shall be seeing	1. we shall be seeing
	2. you will be seeing	2. you will be seeing
	3. he will be seeing	3. they will be seeing
Present Perfect Tense	1. I have been seeing	1. we have been seeing
	2. you have been see-ing	2. you have been see-ing
	3. he has been seeing	3. they have been see-ing
Past Perfect Tense	1. I had been seeing	1. we had been seeing
	2. you had been seeing	2. you had been seeing
	3. he had been seeing	3. they had been see-ing
Future Perfect Tense	1. I shall have been seeing	1. we shall have been seeing
	2. you will have been seeing	2. you will have been seeing
	3. he will have been seeing	3. they will have been seeing

SUBJUNCTIVE MOOD		
Present Tense	1. I be seeing	1. we be seeing
	2. you be seeing	2. you be seeing
	3. he be seeing	3. they be seeing
Past Tense	1. I were seeing	1. we were seeing
	2. you were seeing	2. you were seeing
	3. he were seeing	3. they were seeing

	Present	*Perfect*
INFINITIVES	to be seeing	to have been seeing
PARTICIPLES		having been seeing

210 Conjugation of the Verb SEE — Progressive Form

Passive Voice

INDICATIVE MOOD		Singular	Plural
		1. I am being seen	1. we are being seen
Present Tense		2. you are being seen	2. you are being seen
		3. he is being seen	3. they are being seen
		1. I was being seen	1. we were being seen
Past Tense		2. you were being seen	2. you were being seen
		3. he was being seen	3. they were being seen

211 Besides the tense forms given in 206, 207, 208, two other forms are frequently used: the **progressive** (209, 210) and the **emphatic** (213).

212 The **progressive form** represents action as continuing at the time noted. This form is also called the **present (past, future, etc.) continuous** by many grammarians. It is made by placing some form of the verb *to be* before the present participle (201):

I *am seeing*—you *are seeing*—he *is seeing*.

Although the present-participle form is used in making the progressive verb phrase, the participle is here considered not as a participle but as a part of the entire verb phrase:

David *is painting* a picture. (*Painting*, though present participle in form, is here considered to be a part of the verb phrase *is painting*.)

213 The **emphatic form** gives emphasis to the present or past form of the verb in the active voice (184) by the use of *do, does,* or *did*. Forms of *do* are used also in negative statements and in questions without emphasis:

I *do see.*   She *does see.*   He *did see.* (**emphatic**)
Do you see?   I *do* not see. (**not emphatic**)

214 The **synopsis** of a verb is the correct arrangement of its moods (187–189), voices (184–185), and tenses (191–196) in **one person** (69) and **number** (73); it is an abbreviated conjugation (205).

215 Synopsis of the Verb SEE

in the Third Person, Singular Number

INDICATIVE MOOD	Active	Passive
Present Tense	he sees	he is seen
Past Tense	he saw	he was seen
Future Tense	he will see	he will be seen
Present Perfect Tense	he has seen	he has been seen
Past Perfect Tense	he had seen	he had been seen
Future Perfect Tense	he will have seen	he will have been seen

SUBJUNCTIVE MOOD

Present Tense	he see	he be seen
Past Tense	he saw	he were seen
Present Perfect Tense	he have seen	he have been seen
Past Perfect Tense	he had seen	he had been seen

(The imperative mood is used in the second person only.)

Usage

216 Five frequently used verbs that cause much trouble are the following: *come, go, do, see, give.*

> Bob *came* (not *come*) yesterday.
> He had *come* (not *came*) when I left.
> She had *gone* (not *went*) when you came.
> May *did* (not *done*) the work well.
> She has *done* (not *did*) good work.
> I *saw* (not *seen*) her yesterday.
> Tom had *seen* (not *saw*) the show.
> Ann *gave* (not *give*) me this book.
> Pat had *given* (not *gave*) her a camera.

217 These three pairs of verbs are often confused: *lie—lay, sit—set, rise—raise.*

> *Lie, sit,* and *rise* are always intransitive (175) in their usual meanings. *Lay, set,* and *raise* are usually transitive (174) and, therefore, must have an object to complete the meaning:

Let us *lie* here and rest.	I *laid* the book there yesterday.
She *sits* by the window to read.	I *set* the box on the shelf.
The cake did not *rise* well.	Did you *raise* the flag?

♦ The verbs *lay* and *set* may be used as intransitives in certain of their secondary meanings:

> The hen *lays* well.
> The sun *set* at six o'clock yesterday.
> This jelly did not *set* well.
> We eagerly *set* out on our long journey.

218 *May* is used to express permission; *can* refers to ability:

> May I go to town?   Can the bird fly?

Some writers use *can* for permission, but this usage is more often than not disapproved for written use as being colloquial or informal.

219 Use *shall* in the first person and *will* in the second and third persons for the simple future tense:

> I *shall* sing this afternoon.
> You *will* succeed.   He *will* stay at home.

220 To express determination, desire, or a promise, reverse the normal order and use *will* in the first person and *shall* in the second and third persons:

> I *will* be there.
> You *shall* not go.   They *shall* be brought to justice.

221 In asking questions in the first person, use *shall*; in the second or third person, use the form that would be correct in the answer:

> *Shall* you leave tomorrow? (The answer is "I *shall*.")
> *Will* John defy me? (He *will*.)

222 Use *shall* in all persons in object (noun) clauses after verbs of *deciding, wishing, demanding, willing*, etc.:

> He insists that they *shall* not follow him.

223 In an indirect quotation (expressing the thought but not the actual words of the speaker), use the tense form correct for the speaker:

> John says that he *shall* win. (He said, "I *shall* win.")

224 The uses of *should* and *would* correspond to those of *shall* and *will*:

1. For simple future, use *should* with the first person, and use *would* with the second and third.

2. For determination, reverse the order.

3. In questions in the first person, use *should*. (See 221) In questions in the second and third persons, use the form which would be correct in the answer.

4. In indirect discourse (indirect quotation), use the form that would be correct if the quotation were direct.

♦The rules governing the use of *shall* and *will*, *should* and *would*, are seldom stressed because of a wide variation in actual practice that makes them interchangeable.

225 *Had ought to* is never correct as a combination for *ought to* or *should*:

> He *should* (or *ought to*, not *had ought to*) work.

226 The use of the word *loan* as a verb is interchangeable with *lend* in matters of money but is more restricted in other meanings:

> He *loaned* me ten dollars.   He *lent* his bicycle.

227 Do not confuse *leave* and *let*, *learn* and *teach*. *To leave* means *to go away from; to let* means *to permit* or *to allow*:

She will *let* (not *leave*) us use her pen.

To learn means *to get information; to teach* means *to give information:*

He will *teach* (not *learn*) me to paint.

228 *Accept* and *except* are often confused. *To accept* means *to take; to except* means *to leave out* or *to exclude:*

I *accept* the gift.

If we *except* her picture from the show, she will feel hurt.

229 Although *ain't* is usually condemned as nonstandard, we need some good word to take its place (662):

The roses *aren't* (not *ain't*) in bloom yet.

I am to blame, *am I not* (not *ain't*)?

In England, the form *aren't I* is considered correct in the preceding sentence. Although this form has gained favor in this country, some American authorities still classify it as informal.

230 Never use *of* as a substitute for *have:*

She should *have* (not *of*) gone home.

231 Some authorities object to the formal written use of *and* for *to* with *try:*

Questionable: Try *and* help him.

Correct: Try *to* help him.

However, *and* is never used with *tries, tried,* or *trying.*

232 The *to* is generally omitted from an infinitive (199) that follows certain verbs. Some of the verbs are *bid, dare, let, make, help, need, see:*

Let us (without *to*) go to the show.

233 There is some objection to the use of *but what* for *but that* after negative forms of verbs:

Questionable: He did not know *but what* I left.

Informal: He did not know *but that* I left.

Formal: He did not know *that* I left.

234 Do not use *help but* in the sense of *avoid* in formal writing:

Colloquial: He could not *help but* laugh.

Formal: He could not *help* laughing.

235 The **split infinitive**—the use of a word between the parts of an infinitive (199)—is not at all incorrect, but it usually makes an awkward sentence unless carefully controlled:

Awkward: She told me *to not help* him.
Better: She told me *not to help* him.

Agreement of Verb and Subject

236 Words that are joined to a subject by *with, accompanied by, together with, as well as, no less than,* or *including* do not change the number of the subject:

> The teacher, as well as the students, *was* there.
>
> The students, as well as the teacher, *were* there.

237 Two or more singular subjects joined by *or* or *nor* require a singular verb:

> Neither Esther nor Ruth *was* present.

238 When a subject is composed of both singular and plural forms joined by *or* or *nor*, the verb must agree with the nearer subject:

> Two other boys or Henry *is* to   Neither he nor the boys *play*
> blame!   golf.

239 In a sentence beginning with *here* or *there*, the number of the verb is determined by the number of the substantive following it:

> There *is* a book on the table.   There *are* hats in the window.
> Here *are* Bob and Sue.   There *go* Joe and Fred.

♦ When *there* is used as an introductory word, as in the first two sentences, it is called an **expletive.** An expletive is a word which, without special meaning of its own, introduces a subject or object that follows. *It* is another word frequently used in this way:

> *It* is good to be here.   Make *it* clear that she is invited.

240 A collective noun (59) takes a singular verb when the group is considered as a unit and takes a plural verb when the individuals are considered (92):

> Our football team *is* popular.   The team *have* received their
>   sweaters.

241 In expressions such as *one of the girls who, one of the trees which,* and *one of the persons that,* the verb in the relative clause agrees with the antecedent of the relative pronoun (135):

> He is one of those teachers who *are* inspiring. (The antecedent of *who* is *teachers.*)
>
> She is the only one of the group that *understands.* (The antecedent of *that* is *one.*)

242 *Each, either, neither, someone, somebody, anyone, anybody, everyone, everybody, no one, nobody, one,* and *a person* are singular (163, 164):

> Each of the students *was* (not *were*) questioned.
>
> Neither Rosa nor Tim *was* (not *were*) home.

243 If *plenty* or *rest* is modified by a phrase introduced by *of*, the verb agrees with the noun in the phrase:

> Plenty of potatoes *are* grown in Colorado.
>
> The rest of the jars *are* on the shelf.

♦ Fractions are used in this same way:

> One third of the paper *was* sold.   One fifth of the boats *were* lost.

244 If the word *number* is preceded by *a* and followed by *of*, it takes a plural verb; if it is preceded by *the*, it requires a singular verb:

> A number of men *were* hurt.   The number of accidents *is* great.

245 A noun that refers to an amount of money, a space of time, or a unit of measurement is singular in meaning even though the form is plural:

> Fifty cents *is* the price.   Ten miles *is* a long way to walk.

246 A phrase (389) between the subject (except in the case of a following relative clause as in 241) and the verb does not affect the verb:

> One of the girls *is* my friend.

247 If the subject of a verb is made up of two or more words joined by *and*, the verb is plural. (If the two are thought of as a unit, the verb is singular: Bread and butter *is* a good food.) In asking questions beginning with verbs, it is necessary to be careful:

> Helen and Grace *are* here.   *Are* Grace and her sister here?

248 If a subject consists of two or more nouns, only one of which is expressed, the verb is plural:

> A red and a blue book *are* on the desk.

249 A verb introduced by a relative pronoun (135) has the same number and person as the noun or pronoun to which it refers:

> He gave the book to me who *am* (not *is*) its owner.

Sequence of Tenses

250 If the verb in the main clause (397) is in the past tense (193), the verb in the dependent clause (398) may be in the past tense:

> Jennifer said that she *expected* to go home.

251 The past tense in the main clause (397) may be followed by the present tense in the dependent clause (398) when it expresses a general truth:

Columbus believed that the earth *is* round.

252 An idea once established as truth, now known to be untrue, is expressed in the past tense:

The ancients believed that the earth *was* flat.

253 SEQUENCE OF TENSES IN INDIRECT DISCOURSE (Reported Speech)

        (a) Present or "now" time, or possible future time
        (b) Intended or completed action in past time
        (c) Intended or completed action in future time

1. **Present**
Ben *says* that (a) he *is going* (*goes*) with us.
           (b) he *was going* (*went*) with us.
           (c) he *will be going* (*will go*) with us.

2. **Past**
Ben *said* that (a) he *is going* (*goes*) with us.
           (b) he *was going* (*went*) with us.
           (c) he *will be going* (*will go*) with us.

3. **Future**
Ben *will say* that (a) he *is going* (*goes*) with us.
           (b) he *was going* (*went*) with us.
           (c) he *will be going* (*will go*) with us.

4. **Present Perfect**
Ben *has said* that (a) he *is going* (*goes*) with us.
           (b) he *was going* (*went*) with us.
           (c) he *would be going* (*would go*) with us.

5. **Past Perfect**
Ben *had said* that (a) he *is going* (*goes*) with us.
           (b) he *was going* (*went*) with us.
           (b) he *had been going* (*had gone*) with us.
           (c) he *would have been going* (*would have gone*) with us.

6. *Future Perfect*
Ben *will have said* that (a) he *is going* (*goes*) with us.
           (b) he *was going* (*went*) with us.
           (b) he *had been going* (*had gone*) with us.
           (c) he *would have been going* (*would have gone*) with us.

This chart shows all the possible relationships. Numbers 1, 2, 4, and 5 are used in statement-of-fact situations; numbers 3 and 6 reflect a qualifying or conditional statement which suggests that a clause, such as "if he were asked," has not been expressed though it is implied.

Special Uses of Voice, Tense, and Number

254 Do not shift illogically from the active voice (184) to the passive (185) in the same sentence.

As we came over the hill, we *saw a deer* (not a *deer was seen*).

255 Use the active voice (184) unless there is some self-evident reason for using the passive:

We *heard a noise* (not A *noise was heard*).

256 In expressing a **wish or a condition** contrary to fact, use *were*, not *was*:

If I *were* he, I'd go home.   I wish she *were* the governor.

257 In a past **condition not contrary to fact**, the indicative mood (187) is used, not the subjunctive (189) as in 256:

If John *was* present, I did not see him.

258 After *as if* and *as though*, use the subjunctive *were*:

She speaks as though she *were* angry.

259 With words expressing **command** or **necessity**, use either the present subjunctive form (189) or a verb phrase:

It is necessary that the boy *be* (or *should be*) dismissed immediately.
It was necessary that he *be* dismissed.

260 Use *are* or *were* with *you*, even when the pronoun is singular:

Edgar, you *were* there.   *Are* you there, now?

261 When one subject is affirmative and the other negative, the verb agrees with the affirmative:

Your honesty, not your pleas, *causes* me to relent.

262 In the use of **arithmetical expressions** there has been disagreement as to the correct verb forms, but the following are accepted:

Six divided by three *is* two.	Seven minus two *is* five.
One fourth of twelve *is* three.	Five plus three *is* eight.
Five times two *are* ten.	Three and four *are* seven.

263 When the **infinitive** (199) refers to a time coincident with that of the main verb or some time after it, use the present infinitive:

I intended *to sing* (not *to have sung*).

The **present infinitive** (199, 206) may be used with a main verb in any tense, as follows:

She wishes *to meet* you.	She had wished *to meet* you.
She wished *to meet* you.	She will wish *to meet* you.
She has wished *to meet* you.	She will have wished *to meet* you.

When the **perfect infinitive** (199, 206) is used with a verb in the past tense or in the past perfect tense (193, 194) expressing *desire, hope,* or *duty,* it indicates that something interfered with the desire, hope, or duty:

> She wished *to have seen* you. (She did not see you.)
> I hoped *to have met* you. (I did not meet you.)

When the **present infinitive** is used after one of these verbs there is an element of uncertainty:

> He hoped *to meet* you. (Whether he did or not is uncertain.)

The use of the **perfect infinitive** (199, 206) after such verbs as *seem, appear,* and *know* shows that the event denoted by the infinitive took place before the time indicated by the verb:

> Bob seems *to have succeeded.*

264 It is incorrect to use a present participle when indicating an action previous to that expressed by the main verb:

> He has been away three days, *having left* (not *leaving*) last Monday.

Uses of the Verbals

265 The **infinitive** (199, 232) has many uses:

1. The infinitive used as a **noun** (56, 61.5):
   a. **Subject of a verb** (95): *To win* is not easy.
   b. **Predicate nominative** (96): What she wants is *to win.*
   c. **Object of a verb** (102): He likes *to write.*
   d. **Nominative case in apposition with the subject** (100): His aim, *to succeed,* is commendable.
   e. **Objective case in apposition with the object** (111): She has one great desire, *to succeed.*

2. The infinitive used as an **adjective**: The house *to be sold* is new.
3. The infinitive used as an **adverb**: Mary came *to see* us.

DIAGRAM—An infinitive used as subject:

> *To succeed* is his intention.

266 The gerund (56, 61.4, 200) has many noun uses, as follows:

   1. **Subject of a verb:** *Stealing* is wrong.
   2. **Object of a verb:** I heard the *roaring* of the river.
   3. **Object of a preposition:** Were they punished for *cheating?*
   4. **Apposition:** His work, *mining,* was dangerous.
   5. **Predicate nominative:** Her work is *painting* signs. (*Signs* is object of gerund.)

DIAGRAM—A gerund used as **subject** (266.1) and having an object:

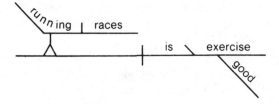

DIAGRAM—A gerund used as an **object** (266.2) and having an object:
The boys dislike *picking* berries. (*Berries* is object of *picking.*)

267 Most authorities agree that a verbal may be considered a pure noun when it has lost the verbal idea; when it may be pluralized; when it may be preceded by an article and followed by a preposition; or when it is the name of an art, a course of study, or some form of activity:

   We attended the *wedding.*   The *rowing* of the boat was easy.
   I know Bob's *drawings.*   I am taking a course in *writing.*

268 A **compound gerund** is formed by placing a noun before a gerund:
mountain climbing, skin diving

   The gerund is also called **verbal noun** or **participial noun** (200).

   ♦ There are some grammarians who believe there is a difference between the gerund and the verbal noun, but the difference is one of identification rather than of use and function.

269 The **participle** is a verbal (198, 201) which is used as an adjective. It has the same uses as the regular adjective (275):

1. **Attributive** (276):
   The *running* stream is beauti-   A *broken* limb of the tree has
   ful.   fallen.

2. **Predicate adjective** (179.4, 278, 289):
   The game was *thrilling*.   The boy is *discouraged*.

3. **Appositive adjective** (277):
   The girl, *running* swiftly, soon disappeared.
   The limb, *broken* by the wind, has fallen down.

The participle ending in *ing* sometimes seems to be a pure adjective, and at other times it is thought of as a part of the verb phrase in the progressive form (212):

The *gleaming* stars are beautiful. (resembles a pure **adjective**)

The stars, *gleaming* in the sky, are beautiful. (**regular participle**)

The stars are *gleaming* in the sky. (**part of the verb**)

The past participle (201) is sometimes used as an adjective and sometimes as the main part of the verb in the passive voice (185):

This drama, *written* by Thornton Wilder, is my favorite. (**adjective**)

This book *was written* by Rachel Carson. (**part of the passive verb form**)

DIAGRAM—A participle (201) having an object:

John, *fearing defeat*, encouraged his comrades.

270 A noun or pronoun introducing a gerund is its subject; it is usually written in the possessive case (116, 127):

He approved *Ann's* (not *Ann*) selling the book.

He did not like *my* (not *me*) going away.

This rule is not rigidly observed in conversation and informal writing.

♦ It will sometimes require close observation to distinguish the participle from the gerund:

We referred to the girl *playing* tennis. (**participle**)

We referred to the girl's *playing* tennis. (**gerund**)

271 A **participial phrase** (390.3) or a **prepositional gerund phrase** should have a substantive (47) that it can logically modify expressed in the sentence. When the substantive is omitted, the modifying phrase is said to be **dangling**. Dangling modifiers often result in absurdities. Be sure to give modifiers something to modify (451):

Running to the window, I saw a fire (not a *fire was seen*). (390.3) (The participial phrase *running to the window* modifies *I*. The fire was not running to the window.)

By working hard, we finished the task (not the *task was finished*). (390.4) (The prepositional phrase *by working hard,* which has a gerund as the object of the preposition, modifies *we*).

Sitting in the moonlight, we enjoyed the music (not the *music was enjoyed*).

♦ A few set phrases, such as *generally speaking, considering every-thing,* are understood to modify the entire sentence, not any particular substantive in it; they are then called **sentence modifiers.**

Punctuation of participles and gerunds is very important. Note the use of the comma (499) in the examples just given. If a participial phrase begins the sentence, it is followed by a comma:

Running quickly, the girl won the race.

The absolute construction (99) is set off from the rest of the sentence by a comma or commas:

The game being ended, we went home.

Sometimes the word *being* is omitted from the absolute construction, but the comma is used:

The matter (being) *adjusted,* we felt relieved.

Nonrestrictive phrases (phrases not necessary to the meaning of the rest of the sentence) are set off by commas (499):

The man *sitting by the desk* is the principal. (**necessary**—no commas used)

The old man, *sitting at the chess board,* planned his next move. (**unnecessary**—commas used)

272 The **subject of an infinitive** (108, 199) is in the objective case:

We asked *him* to go. (*Him* is the subject of *to go.*)

Jack asked *her* to sing. (*Her* is the subject of *to sing.*)

273 In an **infinitive clause** (401), a predicate noun (96) or a predicate pronoun (145.2) used after *to be* is in the objective case to agree with the subject of the infinitive (109):

You thought us to be *them.*

They took me to be *her.*

274 If the infinitive *to be* has no subject, the predicate noun or the predicate pronoun following it is in the nominative case (109):

> He was thought to be *I*.
> I was believed to be *she*.

Adjectives

275 An adjective is a modifier (7) that describes or limits a substantive (47). It may be a word or a group of words (7, 8, 9, 42):

> We saw *beautiful* flowers.
> *Those* flowers *on the desk* are roses. (*Those* is a simple modifier; the group *on the desk* is a phrase modifier, 390.1.)
> *Those* boys *whom you saw* are students. (*Those* is a simple modifier; the group *whom you saw* is a clause modifier, 408.)

The adjective is used effectively in painting word pictures—describing (553). Note the effect of the added modifiers (7) in the illustrations below:

> Near the house stood a tree. (**unimpressive**)
> Above the gray, old-fashioned, stone dwelling a tall, slender eucalyptus tree waved its feathery branches in the summer morning sunlight. (**vivid**)

Adjectives are used in three ways: in **attributive** and **appositive** positions, and as **predicate adjectives.**

276 The **attributive** use of the adjective is that of the direct modifier that precedes the substantive:

> The man wore a *dark* suit.

◆ Adjectives in a series are separated by commas (505):

> A *beautiful, tall, slender* pine stood nearby.

277 The **appositive** use of the adjective directly follows the substantive that it modifies:

> The speaker, *tall* and *graceful*, soon won the audience. (The adjectives *tall* and *graceful* explain the appearance of the speaker. The adjective used appositively is set off by a comma or commas.)

278 The **predicate** use of the adjective (179.4, 289) is to complete the meaning of the predicate and modify the subject:

> The work was *difficult*.   Mountains are *beautiful*.

The predicate adjective is usually joined to the subject by a linking verb (180). (But also see 289.)

279 An adjective that describes a substantive (47) by expressing some quality belonging to it is called a **descriptive adjective:**

> We saw *tall* trees.   They climbed *high* hills.

Noun

280 An adjective that describes a substantive or that limits its meaning without expressing a quality is called a **limiting, or definitive, adjective:**

> She sent us *those* books.   We saw *many* trees.

281 The limiting, or definitive, adjectives include **pronouns used as adjectives** (pronominal adjectives, both indefinite and demonstrative, 138, 139, 140), **numeral adjectives**, and the **articles.**

Pronouns in the possessive case (116, 117) are sometimes called **possessive adjectives** (131, 146):

> John lost *his* book.

♦ The possessive adjective is also pronominal (140).

The **pronominal adjectives** (140) are discussed with pronouns (131, 138, 139), but further illustrations of their uses are given here. Be sure to distinguish between the pronoun use and the adjective use:

> *This* book is a grammar. (**adjective**)
> *This* is a book. (**pronoun,** 138)
> *Each* should bring a book. (**pronoun**)
> *Each* student should bring a book. (**adjective**)
> We saw *her* at the movies. (**pronoun in the objective case**)
> We saw *her* book on the desk. (**pronoun in the possessive case:** also called a **possessive adjective,** 131)

282 **Numeral adjectives** indicate number. There are two classes which are generally used: **cardinal** and **ordinal.**

283 The **cardinal** number indicates how many items there are in a group, or set:

> We saw *three* ships.

284 The **ordinal** number gives the order of the items in a sequence:

> He won the *third* prize.

285 The adjectives *a, an,* and *the* are called **articles.**

286 *A* and *an* are called **indefinite articles** because they do not point out particular persons, places, or things:

> The camper saw a deer and *an* eagle. (*An* is used before a word beginning with one of the vowel sounds—*a, e, i, o, u.* Before a consonant sound, *a* is used.)

287 *The* is called the **definite article** because it points out a particular member of a class of persons, places, or things:

> This is *the* book we need.

♦ *The* may also be used to indicate a generalized noun as a representative of its class:

> We have now studied *the* noun, *the* verb, and *the* adjective.

288 The **proper adjective** is derived from a proper noun (55) or is a proper noun used as an adjective and is written with a capital letter.

Although he is a *British* student, he enjoys the *Colorado* climate.

289 A **predicate adjective** (278) completes the verb and relates to the subject:

She looks *cheerful.*

Predicate adjectives are used with the linking verbs, such as *be* and *become* and such verbs of the senses as: *seems, appears, looks, tastes, feels, smells, sounds;* also *proves, remains, turns, grows, stays, continues.* Avoid substituting an adverb (316) for an adjective after a linking verb (180):

The rose smells *sweet* (not *sweetly*).

He looks *bad* (not *badly*) since his illness.

♦ Predicate adjectives (and predicate nominatives, 96) may also occur after certain verbs (104) in the passive (185):

She was considered *intelligent.*

Predicate objectives, or **objective complements,** may be adjectives as well as nouns (104, 179):

I found her a *job.* (**noun**)   I found her *pretty.* (**adjective**)

290 Many words commonly used as **pronouns** may be used as modifying **adjectives** (138, 139, 281):

That hat is made of fur.   I know *what* man you mean.

Which horse is yours?   *Any* boy can do *that* work.

♦ When the noun that is modified is omitted, each of the adjectives of this class becomes a pronoun (138, 139, 281):

That is made of fur. (**pronoun**)

Comparison of Adjectives

291 Adjectives have **three degrees of comparison: positive, comparative,** and **superlative.**

292 The **positive degree** expresses a quality without comparison:

Joe is *tall.*

293 The **comparative degree** expresses a higher or lower degree than the positive when two persons or things are compared:

Kay is *taller* than Joan.   Joan is *less talkative* than Kay.

294 The **superlative degree** is the highest or lowest degree when more than two persons or things are compared:

Bob is the *tallest* boy in the   He is also the *least talkative*
club.   member.

295 Comparison is indicated in three ways:

   1. By adding *er* or *est* to the positive degree: *large—larger—largest.*

   2. By prefixing *more* and *most* or *less* and *least*: *graceful—more graceful—most graceful; practical—less practical—least practical.*

   3. By irregular inflection (48): *bad—worse—worst.*

Forms of Comparison

Positive	*Comparative*	*Superlative*
long	longer	longest
beautiful	more beautiful	most beautiful
beautiful	less beautiful	least beautiful
much	more	most

296 Use the comparative degree (293), not the superlative, in comparing two objects:

   He is the *older* of the two boys.   She is the *more gifted* of the two.

   ♦ The familiar expression, "Put your *best* foot forward," is correct as an idiomatic construction (664).

297 Certain adjectives that express **absolute qualities** do not logically, and in the strictest sense, admit of comparison; but many good writers do compare them regularly while others use *more nearly* and *most nearly* as an alternative use. The words *unique, perfect, square, straight, endless, dead, perpendicular* are in this group:

   This is the *most* perfect rose. (questionable as **redundant**)

   This is the *most nearly* perfect rose. (preferred as **logically acceptable**)

   However, when such words are not used with their basic literal meaning, they may be compared:

   This is the *deadest* party I ever attended.

298 The comparative is used with *than* because only two things (whether individuals or groups) are involved:

   The new machine runs *faster* than the old one. (Two groups are compared.)

   When comparing something with the rest of the class of things to which it belongs, use *other, else*, or some such word:

   John works faster than any *other* boy in school. (John is compared with the rest of the boys.)

Usage

299 When a numeral adjective and a noun form a compound adjective, the singular form of the noun is used:

   a thirty-*day* vacation, a five-*foot* fence.

300 When a plural adjective modifies a noun, as a rule the noun becomes plural:

He rode ten *miles* (not *mile*).

301 Words such as *dozen, head, score, gross,* and *hundred* retain their singular form when preceded by an adjective expressing number:

He kept three *head* of horses in his stable.

302 *This* and *that* are the only adjectives inflected for number. *This* and *that* modify singular nouns; *these* and *those,* plural nouns:

I like *this* kind of book and *these* kinds of pencils.

She prefers *those* kinds of roses and *that* kind of aster.

303 *First* and *last,* when used with adjectives that express number, are placed before the adjectives to make the meaning specific:

Omit the *last* ten pages.

304 When two or more adjectives modify the same noun, clarity requires that an article (*a, an,* or *the*) be used before the first adjective only:

a blue, gray, and white bird. (one bird)

305 When two or more adjectives modify different nouns, one expressed and the others understood (248), an article is used before each adjective:

The large and *the* small house are mine. (two houses)

306 *Less* indicates amount; *fewer* denotes number:

We hope for *less* rain this month.

Fewer than twenty girls played ball.

307 The article *a* or *an* is not used after *kind of* or *sort of*:

What *kind of* (not *kind of a*) book is that?

308 When two or more nouns are used to refer to the same person or thing, an article should be used before the first noun only:

The teacher and mayor (one person) of the town was loved by everyone.

309 When nouns used together refer to different persons or things, an article should be used before each noun:

The teacher and *the* minister are popular. (two persons)

310 In comparison use *so* instead of *as* after a negative such as *not*:

She is not *so* tall as Jane. (*So* is used in the negative statement.)

She is *as* tall as Mary. (*As* is used in the positive statement.)

311 Do not use an adjective as an adverb. Do not use *sure* for *surely*, *real* for *really*, *some* for *somewhat*, *different* for *differently*:

> She *surely* (not *sure*) is busy.
>
> He was *really* (not *real*) pleased to help.

♦ Some adverbs have two forms, one with *ly* and one like the adjective. The short form may be used in some sentences:

> Drive *slow*.   He went *slowly* down the street.

312 Remember that verbs of the senses, such as *smell, taste, feel, look*, are generally completed by adjectives, not by adverbs:

> He looks *tired*. (**adjective**, 179.4, 278, 289)

313 After any words used as linking verbs (180), the adjective (278, 289) form, not the adverb, should be used; *be, seem, become, appear, prove, remain, keep, stay, continue*, take adjective forms.

314 The verbs *turn* and *grow* used in the sense of *become* are followed by an adjective:

> The leaves turn *red*.   The clouds grow *dark*.

315 The suffix *-like* may be added to many nouns to form an adjective: *homelike, lifelike, swanlike*.

However, *-like* should not be added indiscriminately to those adjectives for which a word with this meaning already exists.

> **Incorrect:** The flame was *bluelike*.
>
> **Correct:** The flame was *bluish*.

Adverbs

316 An **adverb** may modify a **verb** (170–180), an **adjective** (275–280), another **adverb**, a **verbal** (198–201), a **preposition** (341–346), a **conjunction** (365–369), or occasionally a **substantive** (47, 61):

> She sings *beautifully*. (*Beautifully* modifies the verb *sings*.)
>
> He is a *very* great orator. (*Very* modifies the adjective *great*.)
>
> She smiled *rather* sadly. (*Rather* modifies the adverb *sadly*.)
>
> By working *faithfully*, she won success. (*Faithfully* modifies the gerund *working*.)
>
> The little boy, smiling *happily*, ran to meet his father. (*Happily* modifies the participle *smiling*.)
>
> She has learned to write *clearly*. (*Clearly* modifies the infinitive *to write*.)
>
> He was *almost* under the tree. (*Almost* modifies the preposition *under*.)
>
> She came *just* before I left. (*Just* modifies the conjunction *before*.)
>
> *Nearly* all of them were lost. (*Nearly* modifies the indefinite pronoun *all*, see 139.)

The *newly* rich were not invited. (*Newly* modifies the noun equivalent *rich*; see 61. Compare 714.)

♦ Not all grammarians agree and some state that an adverb may not modify the preposition alone, but modifies the entire phrase introduced by the preposition. They also say that an adverb may not modify a conjunction, but modifies the clause introduced by it. Therefore in the sentences above it could be said that *almost* modifies the phrase *under the tree*, and that *just* modifies the clause *before I left*. Sometimes an adverb appears to modify an entire sentence and is therefore called a **sentence adverb**:

Evidently, he doesn't care what we think.

The adverb may be a single word, a phrase (8), or a clause (9):

The child sang *joyfully*. (**word**)

The child sang *with joy*. (**phrase**)

The child sang *because he was happy*. (**clause**)

The addition of adverb modifiers gives life to expression, as is shown by the illustration below (see also 275):

The president spoke.

The new president spoke *briefly* but *enthusiastically* about the plans for the coming year.

Such expressions as *one by one*, *by and by*, *now and then*, and *little by little* are called **phrasal adverbs**.

317 According to their use in a sentence, adverbs may be grouped into three classes: **simple, interrogative,** and **conjunctive.**

318 A **simple adverb** is a simple modifier:

She spoke *kindly*.

319 An **interrogative adverb** is used in asking a question:

Where have you been?

320 A **conjunctive adverb** is used to connect independent clauses (367, 397). Some common conjunctive adverbs are: *accordingly, also, anyhow, besides, consequently, however, moreover, nevertheless, otherwise, still, then, therefore, yet*:

Joe did not like the course; *nevertheless*, he worked hard and made a good grade.

Joe did not like the course; he worked hard, *nevertheless*, and made a good grade.

A semicolon (490) is used between clauses joined by a conjunctive adverb whether the adverb begins the second clause, as in the first sentence above, or is used within it, as in the second sentence.

321 **Simple adverbs are divided into classes: adverbs of manner, time, place, degree, and number.**

322 Adverbs of **manner** indicate how the action takes place:
He walked *proudly*.

323 Adverbs of **time** indicate when the action takes place:
Fred left *yesterday*.

324 Adverbs of **place** indicate where the action takes place:
Some of my friends live *there*.

325 Adverbs of **degree** indicate how much or to what extent:
She seemed *rather* confident.

326 Adverbs of **number** indicate order or how many times:
He arrived *first*.   He came only *once*.

327 Adverbs, like adjectives, have **three degrees** of **comparison** (291–295) —**positive, comparative,** and **superlative:** *slowly—more slowly—most slowly*. In general, only adverbs of manner can be compared.

Usage

328 Do not use the adjective *most* for the adverb *almost* (671):
It seems that *almost* (not *most*) all the students are here. (See 316 and 325)

329 *Good* is an adjective; *well* is usually an adverb. Do not confuse these words:
He writes *well* (not *good*).   The apple tastes *good*. (See 289)
When it means "not sick," *well* is an adjective:
I am glad he is *well* again.

330 Do not use these nonstandard, dialectal adverbial expressions: *anywheres, nowheres, somewheres, nowhere near, illy, muchly.*

331 When *very* or *too* modifies a past participle (201), it should be accompanied by another adverb, such as *greatly* or *much*.
John was very *much* excited.
♦ The adverb *very* is overused as an intensifier and should be avoided. *Very excited* is colloquially acceptable.

332 Do not use such words as *up* and *of* unnecessarily:
Let's *connect* (not *connect up*) these wires.
They lost all (not *all of*) their money.

333 *Kind of* and *sort of* should not be misused for such adverbs as *rather* and *somewhat*, when this is the meaning intended:
She was *somewhat* (not *sort of*) surprised.

334 Do not use *some* as an adverb in careful writing. Use *somewhat*:
He is *somewhat* better today.

335 *Thisaway* and *thataway* are dialectal forms:

> **Dialectal:** The robbers went *thataway*.
>
> **Standard:** The robbers went *that way*.

336 Do not use two negatives to express one negative idea; for example, do not use *not* with *hardly, scarcely, only, neither, never, no one, nobody, nothing, no,* or *none*:

> There was *no one* at home.

> As a rule, place *not* directly before the word it modifies:

> *Not* every soldier can be a general.

> Some apparently double negatives are correct:

> She was not *unwilling* to   *No one* liked the play, *not* even
>   help.   Jane.

337 Use *from* after *different* and *differently* (361):

> He thinks differently *from* (not *than*) you.

338 Do not use any word between the parts of an infinitive (199, 235) if it results in an awkward expression:

> **Awkward:** He told me to *not* sell the book.
>
> **Correct:** He told me *not* to sell the book.

339 Do not misuse the adjective *easy* for the adverb *easily*:

> We can finish *easily* (not *easy*) by noon.

> ♦ Certain phrases, such as *take it easy, go easy,* are colloquially acceptable.

340 The position of the adverb is rather flexible in English, but sometimes the position of an adverb will change the meaning of a sentence:

> He *only* seems interested in reading. (He is really not interested.)

> He seems interested *only* in reading. (Reading is apparently his only interest.)

Prepositions

341 A **preposition** (44) is a word or a word group that shows the relation between its object (106) and some other word in the sentence:

> The eagle soared *above* the peak. (*Above* is a preposition; *peak* is the object of the preposition. The two together form a prepositional phrase.)

> ♦ A word ordinarily used as a preposition may be used as a simple adverb (316, 318) when it has no object, or it may become part of a two-word idiomatic verb such as *get by, fall down,* or *give up.*

> We have met *before*. (**adverb**)
>
> John arrived *before dinner*. (**preposition**)
>
> Send *in* the clown. Send the clown *in*. He was sent *in*. (**part of verb**)
>
> We ran *out* of supplies. (**part of verb**)

342 Although prepositions are variously classified, it is sufficient to know four general classes: **simple, compound, participial,** and **phrasal.**

343 A simple preposition is made up of one word: *by, for, in, with, on.*

344 A compound preposition is made up of two words used as one: *without, upon, into, before, inside, throughout, underneath, outside.*

345 A **participial preposition** is the present participle of certain verbs used with the function of a preposition: *regarding, excepting, respecting, barring.*

346 A **phrasal preposition** is a phrase used as a preposition: *in spite of, in accordance with, with regard to, from below, over against, from among, from between, from under, out of, round about.*

347 Some of the words most frequently used as prepositions are *aboard, about, above, across, after, against, along, amid, among, around, at, before, behind, below, beneath, beside, between, beyond, by, down, during, except, for, from, in, into, of, off, on, over, round, since, through, to, unto, under, up, upon, with,* and *within.*

348 A preposition and its object (with the modifiers of the object) form a phrase (8) which has the use of an adjective (275) when it modifies a noun or a pronoun, and the use of an adverb (316) when it modifies a verb, adjective, or an adverb:

> The tree *in the park* is an oak. (**adjective phrase** modifying *tree*)
>
> We walked *beside the river*. (**adverb phrase** modifying *walked*)

♦ Some linguists state that a prepositional phrase may be used as a noun (47, 61). The following is an example:

> *At the door* was where he left them.

Usage

349 There are some two hundred and eighty-four words and phrases in English used as prepositions and prepositional phrases. The following sections (350–364) illustrate a number of the distinctions to be made in correct usage. Modern dictionaries carefully indicate the idiomatic distinctions to be made in formal expression.

350 One may *agree to* a thing and *agree with* a person:

> I *agree* to the plan.   You *agree* with me.

351 One may be *angry at* or *about* a thing and *angry with* a person:

> I was *angry at* the discourtesy.   He was *angry with* me.

352 One *arrives in* a large city, *at* a small place:

> He *arrived in* Chicago.   We *arrived at* the village.

353 *Besides* means *in addition to; beside* means *by the side of*:

> There were two boys *besides* Henry.   He sat *beside* me.

354 As a rule, *between* refers to two; *among*, to more than two:

> She divided the candy *between* the two boys.
> He threw the confetti *among* the crowd.

355 Use *between* for more than two, however, to express the relationship of one thing or person to any number of others considered individually or severally.

> The choice for the lead part is *between* Amy, May, and Sue.

356 Do not use *inside of* for *within*:

> Olga did the work *within* (not *inside of*) a week.

357 *Into* denotes entrance; *in* denotes location:

> He jumped *into* the water.   He swam *in* the river.

358 One may die *of* disease, *from* exposure, or *by* violence:

> He died *of* pneumonia.   She died *from* exposure, not *by* her own act.

359 *By* is the word to use after *follow* when referring to what follows:

> The murderer was followed *by* a mob.

360 *Differ with* means *disagree in opinion*; *differ from* means *be unlike* or *dissimilar*:

> I *differ with* you about the value of the painting.
> The horses *differ from* each other in color.

361 *From* should be used with the adjective *different*:

> This hat is different *from* (not *than*) that. (337)

362 One *parts from* a person, *with* a thing:

> Romeo *parted from* Juliet.   The miser would not *part with* his gold.

363 Do not use *in back of* for *behind*:

> The garage is *behind* (not *in back of*) the house.

364 Do not use unnecessary words such as: accept *of*, off *of*, remember *of*, where *at*, where *to*.

Conjunctions

365 A **conjunction** (45) connects words or groups of words; in form it may be a single word or a group of words:

> Robert *and* James are here. (a single word connecting two words)
> She came *while* you were away. (a single word connecting clauses)
> The teachers *as well as* the students had a good time. (a group of words used as a conjunction)

366 Although conjunctions have many classifications, it is sufficient for our purpose to note only three general classes: **coordinating, subordinating,** and **correlative.**

Relative adverbs used as conjunctions are also called **conjunctive adverbs** or **adverbial conjunctions.**

367 A **coordinating conjunction** connects two words, two phrases, or two clauses of equal rank:

Paul *and* Carl are here. (*And* connects two nouns.)

She liked to read *but* not to write (not *writing*). (*But* connects two infinitives.)

The coordinating conjunctions in most general use include *and, but, for, or, nor, yet.* The conjunctive adverbs, such as *however, then, therefore,* and *thus,* also connect independent clauses (320).

368 A **subordinating conjunction** connects two clauses of unequal rank; that is, it joins a dependent (subordinate) clause (398) to the independent clause (397) on which it depends:

I was here *before* you came.

Some of the subordinating conjunctions are *as, as if, because, before, if, since, that, till, unless, when, where, whether.*

The relative pronouns *who, whom, whose, which, what, that,* also serve as subordinating conjunctions (135).

369 Conjunctions that are used in pairs are called **correlative conjunctions** and include *both-and, either-or, neither-nor, not only-but also.*

Neither John *nor* I will be able to come.

Usage

370 Do not use *except* for *unless:*

We will play *unless* (not *except* or *without*) you object.

371 Do not use *without* for *that:*

I never meet her *that I do not* (not *without I*) admire her wit.

372 Do not use *like* for *as, as if, as though,* or *that* in formal writing:

Walk *as* (not *like*) he told you.

It seems *that* (not *like*) he should help.

373 *And etc.* for *etc.* is incorrect. *Etc.* is an abbreviation of the Latin words *et cetera,* meaning *and so forth;* therefore, *and* is not needed.

374 *And, but,* and *or* are used so frequently that a piece of writing may soon become overloaded with compound sentences. Learn to use the other conjunctions for sentence variety.

375 *And, or, but,* and correlative conjunctions (369) should be used to join expressions that are parallel in form:

She liked *to stroll* on the beach and *to watch* the sea birds.
He is coming *with us* by car or *with his family* by train.

376 Most grammarians agree that the relative (conjunctive pronoun) *which* should not be used to refer to an entire clause (166):

Questionable: The traffic was heavy, *which* caused me to be late.
Better: I was late because the traffic was heavy.

377 When a subordinating conjunction (368) introduces two or more statements of equal importance, the conjunction should in most cases be repeated before each clause to make the meaning clear:

She told me *that* she had won the prize and *that* she would return.

378 *Nor* is used with *neither*. After a negative word, *nor* introduces an alternative and negates it.

He can *neither* read *nor* (not *or*) write.
He cannot dive, *nor* does he like to swim.

379 After verbs of *saying, thinking,* and *feeling,* do not use *as* to replace *that:*

I feel *that* (not *as*) I should not go.

380 Do not use *where* for *that:*

I read in the paper *that* (not *where*) the price of wheat had advanced.

381 Do not use *if* for *whether* in formal writing:

I do not know *whether* (not *if*) he will come.

382 Each of a pair of correlative conjunctions (369) should be placed immediately before the word it connects:

He eats *both* meat *and* fish. (not: He *both* eats meat *and* fish.)

383 In clauses of purpose, do not use *so* for *so that* in formal use:

He worked hard so *that* he could pay his debts.

384 Use *when* to follow *scarcely* or *hardly;* use *than* to follow the expression of a comparison:

He had scarcely started *when* the accident happened.
He did better *than* I expected.

385 Use *that* before a clause that follows a verb of *saying, thinking,* or *feeling* when the verb is followed by an infinitive:

He studied hard, for he knew *that* to fail would be his ruin.

386 Do not omit *as* when it is necessary to complete a comparison:

Illogical: Jane is tall, if not taller than you.
Logical: Jane is *as* tall *as* you, if not taller.

3

The Sentence

It has been well said that good English is lucid English. If this be true, then the speaker or writer who has mastered the English sentence in its simple and in its complex forms will have the means of self-expression with clarity and precision. In modern terms, one communicates.

Just as a carpenter studies the materials and tools in order to best build a house, we study the sentence as the tool of effective expression for our thoughts.

Sentence Structure and Analysis

387 A sentence must express a thought (1); therefore, it must have a subject and a predicate (3, 4) either expressed or understood (5); and it may also have modifiers (7) and independent elements (12).

In general, sentences are made up of **words, phrases** (8), and **clauses** (9). The classification of words has been given in Chapter Two under *Parts of Speech*. Phrases and clauses are also classified in several ways.

389 A **phrase** is a group of related words used as a part of a sentence but not having a subject (3) or a predicate (4). A phrase may be a modifier (7), a connective (11, 365), or a substantive (47):

Ann came *with me*. (**modifier**)

To make a mistake is not disgraceful. (**substantive**)

The **verb phrase** (15, 41, 181, 391) is not a modifier, a connective, or a substantive.

390 According to **structure** there are four general classes of phrases: **prepositional, infinitive, participial,** and **gerund:**

1. A **prepositional phrase** includes a preposition (341, 347) and its object and modifiers of the object:

   Burns lived *among the hills.*

2. An **infinitive phrase** includes an infinitive and its object or complement and modifiers:

   Byron liked *to write poetry.*

3. A **participial phrase** includes a participle and its object and modifiers:

   The girl, *walking quickly,* joined the others.

4. A **gerund phrase** includes a gerund and its object and modifiers:

   Painting beautiful pictures is interesting work.

391 The **verb phrase** is a phrasal verb, that is, a verb consisting of two or more words (41). The various forms of *be, have* and *do,* and of the other auxiliary verbs (*can, may, shall, will, must, ought*) are combined with main verb forms to make up the verb phrase.

392 According to their **use** phrases are classified as follows: **noun** (substantive), **adjective,** and **adverb.** They are referred to by some writers as **nominal, adjectival, adverbial.**

393 A **noun phrase** may be used as a regular noun, with the exception that it is never used in the possessive case (116):

   Playing tennis is delightful exercise. (This is a gerund phrase, 390-4, used as the subject. All gerunds are, of course, used as nouns, 200.)

   The following sentences illustrate other uses of gerund phrases:

   My favorite exercise is *playing volley ball.* (**predicate nominative,** 96)

   Robert likes *collecting butterflies.* (**object of verb,** 102)

   We talked about *pickling peaches.* (**object of a preposition,** 106)

   Her work, *writing stories,* is very interesting. (**apposition with the subject,** 100, 101)

   He likes his work, *teaching music.* (**apposition with object of verb**)

   The following sentences illustrate noun uses of the infinitive phrase (390.2):

   To learn astronomy is my ambition. (**subject**)

   I like *to collect rocks.* (**direct object**)

   Her desire is *to become a doctor.* (**predicate nominative**)

   Her aim, *to become a doctor,* is worthy. (**apposition with subject**)

   I dread my task, *to sell tickets.* (**apposition with object of verb**)

   He spoke of his duty, *to oppose dishonesty.* (**apposition with object of preposition**)

The prepositional phrase (390.1, 348) is not regularly used as a noun, but some writers consider the following as an example of such a use:

Over the fence is out.

♦ The participial phrase (390.3) is used as an adjective and not as a noun; but the gerund is in reality a form of participle used as a noun and is sometimes called **verbal noun** or **participial noun** (56, 200).

394 An **adjective phrase** is a phrase used as an adjective (42, 275-290, 399). The prepositional phrase (390.1), the infinitive phrase (390.2), or the participial phrase (390.3) may be used as an adjective:

The house *on the hill* is white. (**prepositional phrase** used as an adjective to modify *house*)

Evelyn has a great deal of work *to do*. (**infinitive phrase** used as an adjective to modify *work*)

The girl *holding the bat* is Susan. (**participial phrase** used as an adjective to modify *girl*)

395 An **adverb phrase** is a phrase used as an adverb (43, 316-326, 413). Phrases used as adverbs are generally either prepositional or infinitive:

Helen came *with Mary*. (**prepositional phrase** used as an adverb to modify *came*)

The men came *to work*. (**infinitive phrase** used as an adverb to modify *came*)

♦ Whether a phrase is adverbial or adjectival depends on its use:

He saw a book *on the table*.   He knew the book *on the table*.

396 A **clause** is a group of words which contains a subject (3) and a predicate (4). It is usually considered a part of a sentence; but when it is capable of standing alone, it is equivalent to a simple sentence (21). Words are sometimes properly omitted from the clause (10):

Mary is the girl *who wrote the letter*.

The officer said, "*Stop*." (*You*, the **subject**, is omitted here.)

Clauses as parts of a sentence are classified as **independent** (called also **principal**, or **main, clause**) and **dependent**, or **subordinate clause**.

397 The **main**, or **independent**, **clause** is one that makes complete sense when standing alone and that is grammatically complete.

The students deliver papers before they come to school. (The clause *The students deliver papers* could stand alone, as it expresses a complete thought.)

398 A **dependent** (subordinate) **clause** is used as a part of speech in a sentence and usually does not make sense when standing alone:

The students deliver papers *before they come to school.* (The clause *before they come to school* is incomplete in sense when standing alone; here it is used as an adverb and modifies the verb in the main clause.)

399 A **dependent clause** may be used as a **noun**, an **adjective**, or an **adverb**. The **noun clause** may be used in a variety of ways. These uses are illustrated in sections 400–407. **Adjective clauses** and **adverb clauses** are explained in sections 408 and 409.

Noun Clause

400 The **noun clause** is used as subject (3) of a sentence:

What she thought seemed important to him.

401 The noun clause is used as direct or indirect object of a verb:

Don said *that he tried.*   Joe said, "I can't go." (direct objects)

Give *whoever calls* my new address. (indirect object)

♦ An infinitive (199) construction that often replaces a *that* clause is sometimes called an **infinitive clause:**

Ann asked *me to stay.* (*Me to stay* is the direct object of *asked* and the equivalent of *that I should stay.* Note that the subject of the infinitive, *me,* is in the objective case.

402 The noun clause is used as object of a preposition (106):

We talked about *what we would do.*

403 The noun clause is used as predicate nominative (96):

The fact is *that she won the prize.*

404 The noun clause is used in apposition (100) with the subject:

The report *that she won* is correct.

405 The noun clause is used in apposition (101) with the object of a verb:

You made the statement *that she won.*

406 The noun clause is used in apposition with object of a preposition:

I was unaware of the fact *that she won.*

407 The noun clause is used in apposition (100) with the predicate nominative:

The clearest evidence is the fact *that she won.*

Adjective Clause

408 An **adjective clause** is a clause used as an adjective (275, 414). The adjective clause may be introduced by a relative pronoun (135), a relative adverb (such as *where, when, while, why*) or a subordinating conjunction (368). The relative adverbs are also classed as subordinating conjunctions, but when used to introduce adjective clauses,

they have antecedents. In some instances, the word that connects the clause is omitted:

This is the book *that I bought.* (adjective clause, modifying *book,* introduced by the pronoun *that*)

That is the place *where we saw him.* (adjective clause, modifying *place,* introduced by the relative adverb *where*)

Is that the girl *we met yesterday?* (adjective clause omitting the introductory pronoun)

◆ Whether the introductory word is expressed or not, it must be considered as a part of the clause. The omitted word in the last example is *whom,* and it must be considered the object of *met.*

Adverb Clause

409 An **adverb clause** is a clause used as an adverb (316–326, 414). The adverb clause is introduced by a subordinating conjunction (368):

When we had finished our difficult task, we drove through the park. (The subordinating conjunction *when* introduces the adverb clause which modifies the verb *drove.*)

The adverb clause which stands at the beginning of a sentence is followed by a comma (497) unless it is very short and cannot be misread. A comma is usually not used when the main clause (397) stands first:

When we had finished our difficult task, we drove through the park.

After we left the lights were turned on.

We stayed at home *because the weather was unpleasant.* (The subordinating conjunction *because* introduces the adverb clause which modifies the verb *stayed.*)

Sentence Form

410 A sentence (1,387) must have a subject and a predicate (2) and it may have other parts, such as objects, complements, and modifiers of all types (16–19). As to form, a sentence may be classified as **simple** (21), **compound** (22), **complex** (23), and **compound–complex** (20, 416). The **simple sentence** must have but **one** independent clause (397). The subject (3) or the predicate (4) or both (19) may be compound; and the complete sentence may contain any number of phrases, but no dependent clause (398):

The man at the window sent a ticket for John. (This simple sentence contains two phrases.)

John and Melba bought baseballs and bats and packed them in cartons. (This simple sentence contains a compound subject, a compound predicate, a compound direct object, and one phrase.)

Although there are certain parts (2) necessary to every sentence, all sentences are made up of words and groups of words. We have noted the classification of words as parts of speech (38–386) and the classification of groups of words as phrases and clauses (389–409). In the study of the relationships of the parts of the sentence, there are three methods used by grammarians—parsing, analyzing, diagramming—to state or show these relationships.

411 **Parsing a word** is to name the part of speech (38–52) to which it belongs, its modifications, and its construction in the sentence, that is, to give a grammatical description of it:

> Mary paints beautiful pictures.

Mary is a proper noun (55), feminine gender (65), third person (72), singular number (74), nominative case (95), subject of the verb *paints*.

Paints is a regular transitive verb (171, 174), indicative mood (187), present tense (191), active voice (184), third person (72), singular number (74) to agree (197) with its subject *Mary*.

Beautiful is a descriptive adjective (279), positive degree (292), and modifies the noun *pictures*.

Pictures is a common noun (54), neuter gender (66), third person (72), plural number (75), objective case (102), object of the verb *paints*.

412 **Analyzing a sentence** is to state the relation of the parts of the sentence to each other:

> The little child liked the roses in the garden.

This is a simple declarative sentence (21, 25).

The little child is the complete subject (14); *child* is the simple subject (13); *the* and *little* are adjectives modifying *child. Liked the roses in the garden* is the complete predicate (16); *liked,* the simple predicate (15), is completed by the object *roses* (102). The object (6) is modified by the adjective *the* and the adjective phrase (394) *in the garden.*

413 **Diagramming a sentence** is to make a visual picture of the word relationships in it. Other diagrams of the simple sentence are given under 4, 6, 7, 19, 96, 100, 105, 179, 265, 266, 269.

DIAGRAM—A simple sentence (21) with *a prepositional phrase* (390.1) used as an adjective (394):

> The book *on the desk* is blue.

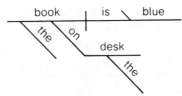

DIAGRAM—A simple sentence with *a prepositional phrase* used as an adverb (395):

A dog ran *under the fence.*

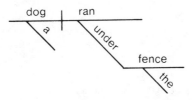

414 A **complex sentence** (23) has but **one** independent clause (397) and one or more dependent clauses (398):

Ruth left *when I arrived.* (*Ruth left* is an **independent clause.** *When I arrived* is a **dependent clause** which modifies the verb *left* as an adverb, 409.)

This is the girl *who wrote the story that won the prize.* (*This is the girl* is an independent clause. *Who wrote the story* is a **dependent clause** that modifies the noun *girl* as an adjective, 408. *That won the prize* is a **dependent clause** that modifies *story* as an adjective.)

The analysis of a complex sentence is similar to that of the simple sentence:

Bob saw the girl who wrote the story. (This is a complex sentence. *Bob saw the girl* is the main, or independent, clause, of which *Bob* is the subject, *saw* is the verb, and *girl* is the direct object. The dependent clause is *who wrote the story; who* is the subject of the dependent clause, *wrote* is the verb, and *story* is the direct object. The dependent clause is an adjective (408), and it modifies the noun *girl.*)

DIAGRAM—A complex sentence with an *adjective clause* (408) introduced by a *relative pronoun* (135) used as *object:*

I saw the horse *that you bought.*

DIAGRAM—A complex sentence with an *adjective clause* introduced by a *relative pronoun* (135) used as *subject*:

The girl *who sat beside me* is my cousin.

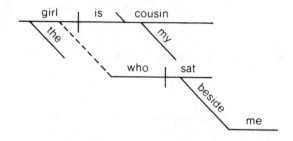

DIAGRAM—A complex sentence with an *adjective clause* introduced by a *relative adverb* (408):

That is the place *where we saw the deer*.

DIAGRAM—A complex sentence with an *adverb clause* (409) introduced by the *subordinating conjunction* (368) *if*:

He will win *if we help him*.

DIAGRAM—A complex sentence with an *adverb clause* introduced by the *subordinating conjunction* (368) *when*:

Mother met us *when we arrived*.

DIAGRAM—A complex sentence with a *noun clause* used as *subject* (400):

That you succeed is the truth.

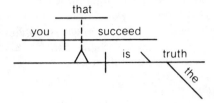

DIAGRAM—A complex sentence with a *noun clause* used as the *object* of a verb (401):

My mother said *that he had won the prize.*

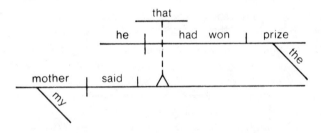

DIAGRAM—A complex sentence with a *noun clause* used as *predicate nominative* or *subjective complement* (403):

The truth is *that he bought the house.*

415 A compound sentence (22) has **two** or **more** independent clauses (397) joined by conjunctions (365–369) or by punctuation (489, 495) or by both:

The little girl went to school, but her brother stayed at home.
The short, friendly little girl went to school; but her brother stayed at home.
The little girl went to school; her brother stayed at home.

When there are no other commas (first example) used in a compound sentence, a comma is placed before the conjunction (495). But when one is used, then the comma is replaced by the semicolon (second example). When the conjunction is not used (third example), a semicolon (489) separates the clauses. The two clauses of the sentence, being independent (397), might stand alone as sentences. But when an independent clause is changed into a sentence, it ceases to be a clause, for a clause by definition is a part of a sentence:

The little girl went to school. Her brother stayed at home. (two simple sentences)

The compound sentence is analyzed in the same way as simple sentences except that the connecting words are mentioned. Every independent clause is practically equivalent to a simple sentence, and a compound sentence may have any number of independent clauses:

The little girl went to school; her brother stayed at home; her father went to his office. (three clauses connected by semicolons, 489)

DIAGRAM—A *compound* sentence:

John goes to college, but Mark stays at home.

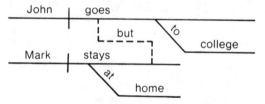

416 If either independent clause of a compound sentence has a subordinate clause (398), the sentence is called **compound–complex,** or **complex–compound:**

When Henry lost the race, he was disappointed; but he was not discouraged.

DIAGRAM—A *compound–complex* sentence:

He lost the knife that he bought, but he may find it.

Sentence Style

417 Sentences are also classified, according to the arrangement of their material, as **periodic**, **loose**, and **balanced**.

418 A **periodic sentence** is one in which the main thought is not given until the end of the sentence is reached. This type of sentence is not grammatically complete until the last word. It lends emphasis:

Today, as never before in the history of the world, we need leadership.

♦ A compound sentence as a whole cannot be periodic, but its parts may be periodic.

419 A **loose sentence** gives the main thought and then adds details. It is the rambling type of expression, much used in conversation:

Lancelot returned with Guinevere in the spring when the flowers were in bloom and the world seemed full of gladness.

420 A **balanced sentence** has two parts which are alike in construction. The thoughts in the two parts may be either in agreement or in contrast:

He told his story at home; then he repeated it at school.

He was always industrious, but he was never successful.

Variety

421 VARIETY IN SENTENCE STRUCTURE   One form of sentence may be just as effective as another, but any form becomes monotonous when it is used too frequently. Valuable practice can be had by expressing similar ideas in sentences of different form:

1. **Simple:** Mary Jones, the efficient president of our class, is an excellent musician. (An appositive, 101, is used.)

2. **Complex:** Mary Jones, who is the efficient president of our class, is an excellent musician. (A dependent, 398, nonrestrictive clause, 499, is used.)

3. **Compound** with a conjunction (415): Mary Jones is the efficient president of our class, and she is also an excellent musician. (A comma, 495, precedes the conjunction.)

4. **Compound** without a conjunction (415): Mary Jones is the efficient president of our class; she is also an excellent musician. (A semicolon, 489, separates the independent clauses.)

5. **Compound–complex** (416): Mary Jones, who is the president of our class, is a very efficient officer; and she is also an excellent musician. (For punctuation, see 489, 491.)

6. **Two simple sentences** (410): Mary Jones is the efficient president of our class. She is also a very good musician.

7. **Three simple sentences:** Mary Jones is the president of our class. She is a very efficient officer. She is also an excellent musician. (Short sentences give emphasis to expresssion, but they tend to become monotonous, 449.)

422 VARIETY IN STRUCTURE PATTERNS Through variety in structure patterns, sentences may be kept free from monotony:

1. **Phrase** (390.3): *Finishing the job,* the people left.
2. **Phrase** (390.3): *Having finished the job,* the people left.
3. **Clause** (398): *The people, who had finished the job,* left.
4. **Clause** (408): *When the people had finished the job,* they left.
5. **Absolute construction** (99): *The job being finished,* the people left.
6. **Absolute construction** (99): *The job finished,* the people left.
7. **Gerund** (56, 200): *After finishing the job,* the people left.

♦ The use of the participial phrase (390.3) to replace the adjective clause (408) lends economy to and often strengthens the statement.

The person *standing beside the gate* is an officer. (**phrase**)
The person *who is standing beside the gate* is an officer. (**clause**)

423 VARIETY IN ARRANGEMENT In arranging material into sentences, it helps to vary the placement of emphasis. The periodic sentence (418) gives emphasis to the important idea in a sentence, but it should not be used either to the exclusion of the loose sentence (419) or, where appropriate, of the balanced sentence (420).

Yesterday afternoon about four o'clock my friend met with a serious accident. (**periodic sentence**)

My friend met with a serious accident yesterday afternoon about four o'clock. (**loose sentence**)

424 VARIETY IN LENGTH The length of sentences should be varied. Short sentences become tiresome when used to excess, and a sequence of long sentences has a tendency to make reading more difficult.

425 VARIETY OF BEGINNING Sentences which begin in the normal order (29) of subject first may become as tedious as any other oft-repeated sentence form; therefore, variety of beginning is important in gaining the reader's attention. The following beginnings suggest various ways of attaining variety.

426 A sentence may begin with a prepositional phrase (390.1):
In those days people loved dangerous adventure.

427 A sentence may begin with a participial phrase (390.3):

Hoping to reach home before the storm, the rider urged his horse forward.

The day being clear, we played tennis. (**absolute, 99**)

428 A sentence may begin with an adverb (316):

Silently and sadly, the old man turned away.

A sentence may begin with an adjective (275):

Beautiful as the trees were, they were cut down for the new building.

429 A sentence may begin with a direct object of a verb (102):

Friends and *enemies* alike he betrayed in order that he might gain wealth.

430 A sentence may begin with a dependent clause (398):

That you are in earnest will help your cause. (**noun, 400**)

When the time comes, we will act. (**adverb, 409**)

431 A sentence may begin with a verb (41) or verbal (198):

Work hard if you wish to succeed.

To succeed is the desire of nearly everyone. (**infinitive phrase, 309.2**)

Helping others gives real joy. (**gerund phrase, 390.4**)

Effectiveness

432 **Effective Sentences** An effective sentence must have **unity, coherence,** and **emphasis.**

433 **Unity** requires that the sentence must express connected thoughts; hence the relationship of thoughts must be clearly shown:

Weak: Fred Smith visited me last summer, and he once lived in England.

Better: Fred Smith, who visited me last summer, once lived in England.

434 **Coherence** requires that the connections between different parts of the sentence be made perfectly clear:

Confusing: Ruth returned the book which she had borrowed last week this afternoon.

Clear: This afternoon Ruth returned the book which she had borrowed last week.

435 **Emphasis,** or force, is given to the main ideas of a sentence by placing them properly in the positions of greatest emphasis—the beginning and the close. Force is given by arranging ideas in order of climax, by repetition of words or sounds, by the use of figures of speech (676), by the addition of modifiers (275, 316), as well as by conciseness of expression (436) and by variety (421–431):

1. Emphasis gained by **position**:
   Poor: After a long search they found the lost child in the woods.
   Better: After a long search in the woods they found the lost child.

2. Emphasis gained by **climax**:

   Flood has brought to these people hunger, disease, death. (See **anticlimax**, 458)

3. Emphasis gained by **repetition**:

   Mr. Smith is a man who is loyal—*loyal* to his friends, *loyal* to his family, *loyal* to his co-workers.

   ♦ The repetition of the same beginning letter or sound, called *alliteration*, is used effectively in advertising: *w*atch, *w*ait, *w*in.

4. Emphasis gained by **figures of speech**:
   a. **Simile** (677): The oak stood *like a sentinel*.
   b. **Metaphor** (678, 679): The rose is *queen* of all flowers.
   c. **Personification** (680): The trees *laughed* in the June sunlight.
   d. **Hyperbole** (681): He gave a *thousand* excuses for his failure.

5. Emphasis gained by **addition of modifiers** (275, 316):

   He is a *handsome, intelligent,* and *rather ambitious* young man.

436 A more **concise expression** sometimes adds force. Conciseness in statement may be gained by changes in form or style:

1. An appositive (101) may be substituted for a sentence:
   Susan Smith addressed the meeting. *She is our president.*
   Susan Smith, *our president,* addressed the meeting.

2. A participial phrase (394) may replace a clause (396):
   The man *who is standing near the desk* is the president.
   The man *standing near the desk* is the president.

   A participial phrase also may be used to replace a sentence:

   The beautiful building was destroyed by fire. *It was completed only a year ago.*

   The beautiful building, *completed only a year ago,* was destroyed by fire.

3. A noun clause (400–407) may replace a sentence:
   Anita is ambitious. *That fact is self-evident.*
   That Anita is ambitious is self-evident.

4. A gerund may make a sentence more concise (200, 266):
   It is my ambition to achieve a deserved success.
   Achieving a deserved success is my ambition.

5. An infinitive may make a sentence more concise (199, 265):

That I may win a deserved success is my ambition.
To win a deserved success is my ambition.

Structure and Style

437 Confusing References   A sentence may be faulty because a pronoun is placed where it may refer to more than one word: There should be no uncertainty as to what word is the antecedent (129) of a pronoun.

438 Confusing reference of the relative pronoun:

Confusing: She left the book on the table that she had just bought from the publisher. (The *that* seems to refer to *table*, though it should refer to *book*.)

Clear: She left on the table the book that she had just bought from the publisher. (The *that* clearly refers to *book*.)

439 Confusing reference of the personal pronoun:

Confusing: Harry told Fred that he would become a great musician. (It is not clear whether *he* refers to Harry or to Fred.)

Clear: Harry said to Fred, "You will become a great musician." OR, Harry said to Fred, "I will become a great musician."

440 An indefinite antecedent (129) of the pronoun:
Confusing: She asked me to help him, but I forgot about it.
(The *it* has nothing definite to refer to.)
Clear: She made a request that I help him, but I forgot about it.
(The antecedent is *request*.)

441 As a rule avoid using *which* to refer to a clause (166, 376):

Ineffective: My uncle came to see me, which pleased me greatly.
Better: I was pleased because my uncle came to see me.

442 Do not misuse *them* for *those:*

I think those (not *them*) roses are lovely.

Do not use *they* with indefinite reference (169):

People (not *They*) say he is honest.

443 Unrelated Ideas   Unrelated ideas should not be placed in the same sentence:

Disconnected: Fred won the race, and he likes chocolate candy.

444 Comma Blunder (*also comma splice* or *fault*)   Two independent clauses (397) not joined by a conjunction should not be separated by a comma unless they make up a series (496). They should be separated by a semicolon (489) or written as two sentences:

Incorrect: We spent the summer in Colorado, we had a good time.
Correct: We spent the summer in Colorado, and we had a good time.
Correct: We spent the summer in Colorado; we had a good time.
Correct: We spent the summer in Colorado. We had a good time.

445 RUN-ON SENTENCES A serious and common writing error is the run-on sentence in which two sentences are written as one without punctuation (35):

Incorrect: We rambled through the woods all day we did not reach home till late.
Correct: We rambled through the woods all day. We did not reach home till late.

446 PERIOD FAULT Through the misuse of the period, students sometimes write fragments for sentences:

Incorrect: We returned home. Hoping to have another picnic soon. (A participial phrase (390.3) is written incorrectly as a sentence.)
Correct: We returned home, hoping to have another picnic soon.
Incorrect: They liked all kinds of games. Especially football.
Correct: They liked all kinds of games, especially football.
Incorrect: We had a good time. When we were in Colorado. (A dependent clause, 398, is written incorrectly as a sentence.)
Correct: We had a good time when we were in Colorado.

♦ Some professional writers occasionally do use the fragment very effectively in their work, but the young writer should construct complete sentences.

447 AND–AND CONSTRUCTION It sounds childlike to join many sentences by *and* as if all the ideas were of equal rank:

Childish: We finished our work, and we went fishing, and we had a good time.
Improved: After we had finished our work, we went fishing and had a good time.

448 OMISSION OF NECESSARY WORDS This common fault occurs in several ways:

1. **Subject of sentence omitted.** The subject should be expressed in a declarative sentence (25) in order to make the meaning clear (33):

Faulty: Went to the football game yesterday.
Correct: I (*or* He, They, etc.) went to the football game yesterday.

In the imperative sentence (26) the subject is correctly omitted:

Correct: Lend me your book.

2. **Subject of dependent clause omitted:**

Not clear: When in Chicago, my father sent me a watch.

Correct: When I was (*or* he was) in Chicago, my father sent me a watch.

Not clear: When ten years old, his mother died.

Correct: When he was ten years old, his mother died.

In elliptical sentences (5) the omission (ellipsis) of words gives strength rather than weakness, especially in the answers to questions.

Welcome. (*You are* welcome.)

Where have I been? At school. (*I have been* at school.)

Do you like Shakespeare's plays? Yes. (Yes, *I like Shakespeare's plays.*)

449 PRIMER SENTENCES Some students fall into the habit of writing monotonous short sentences like those in a primer:

Childish: We went to town. We stayed all day. We came home. We were tired.

Better: After we had spent the day in town, we came home tired.

♦ Short sentences may at times be used effectively, as an element of style, for emphasis.

She planned. She worked. She succeeded.

450 PARALLEL STRUCTURE Parallel thoughts should be expressed in terms that are grammatically parallel:

Faulty: *Swimming* is more enjoyable than *to row*. (One is a gerund and the other is an infinitive.)

Better: *Swimming* is more enjoyable than *rowing*. (Both are gerunds, 200.)

Better: *To swim* is more enjoyable than *to row*. (Both are infinitives, 199.)

451 DANGLING MODIFIERS Modifiers should not be left dangling—with nothing to modify (271). A participial phrase (390.3) or a prepositional phrase (390.1) at the beginning of a sentence relates to the subject of that sentence. A participial phrase at the beginning of a sentence is followed by a comma:

Faulty: Walking down the street, the beautiful building was admired. (The *building* did no *walking*.)

Clear: Walking down the street, we admired the beautiful building.

Faulty: On entering the room, the picture is seen. (There is nothing for the phrase to modify; the *picture* does not do the *entering*.)

Clear: On entering the room, one may see the picture. (The introductory prepositional phrase which contains a gerund modifies *one*.)

452 MISPLACED MODIFIERS   Modifiers—whether they are words (340), phrases, or clauses—should be so placed that their meaning is immediately clear to the reader (438):

> **Confusing:** She almost spent a hundred dollars.
> **Clear:** She spent *almost* a hundred dollars.
> **Confusing:** We saw a man on a horse with a wooden leg.
> **Clear:** We saw a *man with a wooden leg* on a horse.
> **Confusing:** Jane saw a hat in a window that she liked. (438)
> **Clear:** Jane *saw in a window* a hat that she liked.

Shifts in Structure

453   Avoid needless shifts in **person**:
> One must work if *one* (not *you*) would succeed.

454   Avoid needless shifts in **number**:
> One should do *one's* (not *their*) duty.

455   Avoid needless shifts in **voice** (254, 255):
> As we went up the path, *we saw a snake* (not *a snake was seen*).

456   Avoid needless shifts in **tense**:
> The hunter went into the woods and there *he saw* (not *sees*) a deer.

457   Avoid needless shifts in **subject**:
> Ted's letters are interesting, because *they are cleverly written* (not *he is a clever boy*).

Loss of Sentence Effectiveness

458 ANTICLIMAX   The sentence may lose effectiveness from anticlimax, the reverse of climax (435.2), arranging ideas in the order of descending importance:
> Flood has brought to these people *death, disease, hunger.*

459 EFFECTIVE REPETITION   Repetition of words may either strengthen or weaken a composition, depending upon whether important or trivial ideas are repeated.

460   A sentence may be strengthened by repetition of important words or ideas (435.3).

461 MONOTONOUS REPETITION   Avoid the careless repetition of words:
> **Monotonous:** *Autumn* is the most *enjoyable* time of year, because it is in *autumn* that the weather is most *enjoyable.*

Improved: *Autumn* is the most *enjoyable* time of the year, because it is the season when the weather is most pleasant.

462 Wordiness A sentence may lose some of its effectiveness through wordiness—lack of economy in the use of words:

Wordy: He spoke in a very enthusiastic manner to the boys and girls of the high school about the wonderful opportunities of the future which lay ahead of them.

Concise: He spoke with enthusiasm to the high-school students about the opportunities of the future.

Redundancy denotes the use of unnecessary words:

Joe, he works fast.   This here book is good.

Tautology is the needless repetition of an idea in different words:

Refer it back to me.   It is an ancient, old castle.

463 Artificial Expression A sentence may lose in strength because of artificial expression:

Artificial: A vast concourse of those amicably inclined toward him assembled to do him honor on his natal day.

Natural: Many of his friends came to celebrate his birthday.

4

Mechanics
of Composition

One meaning of the word *mechanics* is "Routine procedure; technical details or method." It has been a long time since the advent of printing gave impetus to the standardization of the "technical details" of the English language as we use it today. In so complicated a structure as language, change, of course, is always taking place. But tradition dies slowly, and the usage reported here represents the standards of *American English* for our time. We should not forget that other sectors of the English-speaking world—Great Britain, Canada, Australia, South Africa, the West Indies, for example—may have come to accept usage patterns that vary from that of American usage.

Capitalization

464 Every sentence except a short parenthetical sentence within another should begin with a capital letter:

> The day was beautiful.
> Mary left yesterday (she had been here a week) for New York.

465 In traditional poetry every verse (line) begins with a capital letter:

> What is an epigram? A dwarfish whole;
> Its body brevity, and wit its soul. —COLERIDGE

♦ Some modern poets do not follow this rule.

466 The first word of a direct quotation in reported speech begins with a capital letter:

The girl said, "Wait for me."

467 The first word of a formal statement or resolution following introductory words (often italicized) is capitalized:

Resolved, That the world is growing better.

468 Every proper noun (55) (real or fictional) and every adjective derived from a proper noun (288) should be capitalized: *Boston, Bostonian, Spain, Spaniard; Samuel Johnson, Johnsonian; Miss Universe.*

469 The names of the days of the week, of special holidays, and of the months are capitalized: *Sunday, Memorial Day, June.*

470 Names of the seasons are not capitalized ordinarily (483):

I like summer better than winter.

471 Names of particular associations and proper names resulting from membership in these associations are capitalized: *Republican Party, Republican; Democratic Party, Democrat; Methodist Church, Methodist; Greenville Garden Club; Vermont Historical Association.*

♦ Classes, schools, and colleges are capitalized when they refer to the particular:

John is a senior at Carlyle *College;* he attended Oak Hills *High School.*

The *Junior* Class invited Ms. Smith to speak.

The *Juniors* of 1982 came to the party; freshmen and sophomores were also invited.

School subjects that name languages or that have a particular course number are capitalized, but general subject names are not: *English, Physics II,* but *european history, algebra.*

472 Some abbreviations, such as the following, are written with capitals: A.D. (anno domini); B.C. (before Christ); SW (southwest); R.R. (railroad). Abbreviations of degrees and organizations are capitalized: A.B., M.D., Ph.D.; A.A.A., A.C.S., U.S.A.

473 Important historical events, documents, buildings, and monuments should be capitalized:

Battle of Hastings, World War II, the Declaration of Independence, The White House, Lincoln Memorial.

474 The words *east, west, north,* and *south* are capitalized when they mean particular sections of a country, but they are not capitalized when they mean direction.

He came from the *South*. (**a section of a country**)

He went *south* from town. (**a direction**)

The compounds of these words follow the same rule:

He lives in the great *Northwest*.

Is Hutchinson *northwest* of Wichita?

475 The names of deities, religions, and sacred documents are capitalized: *Allah, Jehovah, Brahma, Zeus, Buddhism, Shintoism, the Koran, the Bible*.

476 Nouns and personal pronouns (132) referring to God or to Christ are capitalized; but some writers do not capitalize the personal pronoun when its antecedent (129) is expressed:

I know *He* is the *Lord*.   Jesus spoke to *his* apostles.

477 Names for the Bible and its parts and books begin with capital letters:

Bible, the Scriptures, Old Testament, Deuteronomy. (Do not italicize such words in running text.)

478 The first, last, and important words in the titles of books, literary articles, pictures, musical compositions, chapters of books, poems, plays, stories, newspapers, and magazines begin with capitals. Prepositions, articles, and conjunctions are usually not capitalized unless they begin the title, but prepositions of five or more letters may be capitalized; a preposition at the end of a title is capitalized. If an article begins the title of a magazine or newspaper, it is not capitalized unless it begins a sentence:

"Ode on a Grecian Urn"   He reads the *New York Times*.

479 The pronoun *I* and the vocative *O* (O Apollo) are always capitalized, but the interjection *oh* is capitalized only when it begins a sentence or stands alone:

Oh, will they come?   *Oh!*

480 The initials of a person's name are capitalized.

481 Titles used with proper names are capitalized:

We think that *Captain Smith* would make a good leader.

He saw *Principal John Moore* at the meeting.

My favorite teachers are Mr. Kovaks and Ms. Evans.

482 When a civil or personal title is used as a proper noun referring to a specific person or thing, it is correct to capitalize it.

Ann went with *Mother* and me to see her mother and father.

Will you help me, *Father*, with my work?

The *Secretary of State* will be named soon.

Our *Federal Government* differs from other federal governments.

483 Common nouns are capitalized when they are strongly personified:

Come, lovely *Spring*, and make us glad.

484 A common noun, such as *river, mountain, park, lake, gulf, ocean, street, avenue, hotel, church, school, club, society, or company,* is properly capitalized when it becomes a part of a particular name:

Is Lowell *School* near Belmont *Park?*

Does Clifton *Avenue* cross Maple *Street?*

Some newspapers vary this rule, as in these examples:

Is Lowell school near Belmont park?

Does Clifton avenue cross Maple street?

But when the common noun precedes the particular name, it is always capitalized:

He lives near *Lake Erie.*

485 It is good practice to refer to a dictionary for the capitalization of words as proper nouns and adjectives. Many words do have correct usage as both common (generic) and proper nouns: *renaissance–Renaissance, revolution–Revolution, ohm–Ohm, watt–Watt.*

Punctuation

Period

486 A period should be placed at the end of every declarative (25) and every imperative (26) sentence unless it is used as an exclamatory (28) sentence or in a sentence used parenthetically within another sentence (464). An elliptical expression (5, 448) used as a substitute for a sentence is followed by a period or other end punctuation:

Jean went to Europe last summer. (**declarative**)

Let me see your new book. (**imperative**)

Annette Jones (she is president of our class) will preside. (**parenthetical sentence** with no capital, 464, and no period) Yes. (**elliptical**)

♦ The polite request expressed in interrogative form so frequent in letters is generally followed by a period, not a question mark (529):

Will you please send your latest catalog.

487 Use periods after a person's initials and some abbreviations (538):

Geo. F. Smith; A.D.; B.C.; A.M.; Mr.; Mrs.; Ms.

There are many exceptions, such as *IQ, DDT.* Abbreviations of many organization names omit periods: *WAFS, WAVES*—especially if they may be pronounced as a word (an acronym)—or they may be written either way:

Y.M.C.A. or *YMCA, USMC* or *U.S.M.C.*

Consult a dictionary as a guide to the handling of abbreviations. Do not use a period after a contraction or after a shortened form of a name used as a part of a whole name:

Ben Brown *isn't* here.

Only one period is necessary at the end of a sentence even when it ends with an abbreviation, but a question mark (529) may follow the period used after an abbreviation at the end of a sentence:

A great battle was fought in the year 490 B.C.

What battle was fought in the year 490 B.C.? (Marathon)

What great siege occurred in A.D. 490? (Ravenna)

488 Three periods are used to show omission in quoted material:

"He did his best . . . yet he never quite succeeded."

Four periods show that a whole sentence (or sentences) has been omitted:

"He said they would come. . . . But they never did come."

489 The period is used between the integral and decimal parts of a mixed fraction and between figures indicating dollars and cents:

The lake is 62.35 miles long. One mile is 1.609 kilometers.

With the discount it will cost $14.22.

Semicolon

490 Use a semicolon between two clauses of a compound sentence (415) when they are not joined by a conjunction (365–369), unless they are very short and are used informally (496).

The rain fell in torrents; we turned everywhere for shelter. (This may be also stated as two sentences.)

He came, he saw, he went away.

The semicolon is used between clauses of a compound sentence that are joined by conjunctive adverbs (320), such as *therefore, hence, however, nevertheless, accordingly, thus, then:*

The day was very cold; therefore, we did not go for a ride.

♦ When used transitionally, conjunctive adverbs are followed by a comma, to show a pause.

491 The semicolon is properly used between clauses that are joined by conjunctions if the clauses are long, or if they have internal commas:

John arrived last night, I am told; but because his plane was late, he could not come to the party.

♦ The semicolon is often used to prevent misreading:

We invited Cindy Webb, the captain of the team; Don Mills, the president of our class; and Joe Wynn, the chairperson of our group.

492 The semicolon usually precedes *as, namely,* or *thus* when used to introduce examples (for a single example a comma suffices):

Four boys were mentioned; *namely,* Henry, Manuel, David, and Clyde.

Only one color was used, *namely,* blue.

Colon

493 The colon is used to introduce formally a word, a list, examples, a statement or question, a series of statements, or a long quotation. An expression such as *the following* often precedes the list:

The following fruits are for sale: apples, peaches, pears.

494 A colon is used after the salutation of a business letter and is used between the parts of a number denoting time:

Dear Sir or Madam: The plane arrives at 6:15 A.M.

Comma

495 The general rule is that a comma is used between the clauses of a compound sentence (415) when they are joined by such conjunctions as *but, for, or, and.*

Robert adjusted the telescope, but I still could see nothing.

I gave the unusual stamps to Karen, for she is a collector.

You may go to a movie, or you may come to the rally with me.

I read about comets, and Laura read about black holes.

♦ When the clauses are very short and closely connected in thought, the comma may be omitted.

I called but he had left.

If the clauses are long and have commas within them, a semicolon should be used to separate them (see 491).

496 Very short clauses making up a series and not joined by conjunctions may be separated by commas (490, 504):

She came, she looked, she went away.

497 An adverbial clause (409) that precedes a main clause (396, 397), unless it is very short, is set off by a comma:

When my cousin came to visit me, she found me at work.

If you expect to succeed, you must prepare yourself.

The comma is usually omitted when the adverbial clause follows the main clause.

My cousin found me at work when she came to visit me.

498 A comma should be used to set off *yes* or *no* used as mild interjections or as sentence adverbs:

Yes, you may go.

Other mild interjections (46), such as *ah, oh, well, why*, are set off by commas when exclamation marks would be too strong:

Ah, well, who can tell what may happen?

499 Nonrestrictive phrases and clauses should be set off from the rest of the sentence by a comma or commas. A nonrestrictive phrase or clause is a nonessential phrase or clause; that is, it is a phrase or a clause that can be omitted without changing the meaning of the main clause (sentences 2, 3, and 6 have a restrictive, or limiting, clause or phrase):

1. Edgar Allan Poe, who wrote "The Raven," was an American writer. (The clause *who wrote "The Raven"* is not necessary to the meaning of the main clause.)

2. Students who study will learn. (The clause *who study* is necessary to explain which students will learn.)

3. The girl who sells the tickets is an honor student. (*Who sells the tickets* is necessary to explain which girl is an honor student.)

4. Jane Gray, *who sells the concert tickets,* is a member of our class. (The clause is not necessary; it merely explains that the girl sells tickets.)

5. The boy, *seeing the clouds,* hurried home. (The phrase is not necessary to explain *boy.*

6. The girl *holding the flag* is Margaret. (The phrase is necessary to tell which girl is Margaret.)

7. *Wishing to see the parade,* we went to town early. (A participial phrase, 390.3, that stands at the beginning of a sentence is followed by a comma.)

8. *The task being done,* we went home. (absolute construction, 99)

Restrictive, or limiting, clauses or phrases are not set apart by punctuation.

500 Items of a parenthetical nature are set off by commas. Two commas are necessary when the expression is within the sentence and no other mark is used. Such items include persons addressed, appositives, and items in addresses, as well as independent phrases and clauses:

Will you help me, *Harry*, with this work?

Nan Gray, *my favorite cousin*, is here.

Tom came from Dallas, *Texas*, yesterday.

That boy is, *I believe*, a dependable fellow.

When an appositive (101) is an attribute, or part, of the proper name or is closely connected with the word it explains, no comma is used:

Edward *the Confessor* was there.   My cousin *Nell* lives in Arizona.

♦Distinguish between appositives preceded by *or*, which usually define, and items that are simple choices. The appositives are set off by commas.

An American bison, *or buffalo*, was given to the zoo. (**defining**)

An adverb may modify an adjective or a verb. (**simple choice**)

501 A direct quotation equivalent to a sentence should be separated from explanatory matter by a comma or commas. But a sentence quoted within another sentence may be so closely connected with the rest of the sentence that no comma is needed:

The girl said, "Wait for me."   "Wait for me," the girl said.

"Wait," the girl said, "until I come."

Her cheerful greeting was always "How do you do today?"

No comma is used before an indirect quotation or a title in quotation marks unless there is a special need for it:

Fred said that he went to Chicago.

Longfellow wrote "The Psalm of Life."

502 Items in a date are set off by commas:

They were married on Tuesday, May 6, 1946.

In a date consisting of month and year only, commas are omitted.

In August 1980, we were on vacation.

503 Use commas for explanatory matter in connection with a direct quotation, unless stronger punctuation is necessary (495):

"It is time," she said, "for me to go home."

"It is time to go," she said; "it is very late."

"It is time to go," she said. "It is very late."

504 Use commas to separate the items of a series of words, phrases, or short clauses:

The farmer sold corn, hay, oats, potatoes, and wheat.

They come from the east, from the west, from the north, and from the south.

He rose, he smiled, he began to speak.

505 A series of adjectives of the same rank modifying the same noun are separated by commas unless they are joined by conjunctions. No comma is used after the last adjective:

> We saw tall, slender, graceful trees.
> He drew the trees as tall, slender, and graceful.
> A steep and narrow path led on.

When the adjective next to the noun seems to be a part of the noun, no comma is used before it:

> He is a courteous young man. (*Courteous* modifies *young man.*)

506 A comma may sometimes be necessary for clarity of meaning:

> Ever since, Frank has been a better boy.
> You would, would you?

Quotation Marks

507 Quotation marks are used to enclose a direct quotation. They are not used with indirect quotations:

> "*You are to blame,*" she said.
> He said *that he would go home.*

508 Quotation marks or italics are used to distinguish words or letters referred to merely as words or letters. (Italics are preferred in printed form for this use.)

> You may parse the words "they" and the two "a's" in that sentence.

♦ Never use quotation marks where they are not required by the rules of composition mechanics. Do not use quotation marks for simple emphasis or for adornment.

509 Quotation marks are used with: the titles of articles; the chapter titles of books; the titles of short poems, songs, and stories; and the parts of a musical composition. (Italics are used in print for titles of books; periodicals; names of ships, airplanes, satellites, spacecraft, etc., 539.)

> He read Whittier's "Maud Muller."
> The article was called "Capturing the Imagination."
> I have read Hawthorne's "Rappaccini's Daughter."
> He listened to the "Third Movement" of the *Ninth Symphony.*

♦ One line drawn under a handwritten or typed word indicates that it would be italicized in print.

510 A long quotation of several paragraphs may have quotation marks at the beginning of each paragraph and at the end of the last paragraph. However, most long quotations are set off by additional indention or by smaller type or by both, and in this case no quotation marks are used in print. (See examples in 544, 548–550, 552, 553, 560.)

511 In reporting conversation, each speech or fragment of speech (515) no matter how short, should be in quotation marks. An uninterrupted quotation in one paragraph, though long, should have but one set of quotation marks (beginning and ending):

"Do you know me?" he asked.

"I am not sure," she replied, "that I have ever met you."

"I am your old schoolmate, Edgar Jones," he explained.

512 Nicknames and words or phrases used ironically may be put in quotations:

My friend "T-Bone" was at the picnic.

His "limousine" was a jalopy. (Be sparing of this use; it may become very annoying.)

♦ Usually quotation marks are omitted from nicknames after the first use or when the nickname (such as *Babe* Ruth) is well known. Many writers also use quotation marks to distinguish technical terms and words used in very specialized meaning.

Often it is better to avoid the use of slang and faulty diction than to apologize for it with quotation marks. Whenever the slang phrase is too expressive to omit, assume responsibility for using it instead of quoting it.

513 A quotation within a quotation should be enclosed in single quotation marks, and a quotation within that should be in double marks:

"I was surprised," Mary admitted, "when he said, 'I agree with Shakespeare, "All the world's a stage." ' "

514 A question mark or an exclamation mark is placed inside the quotation mark if it is a part of the quotation; outside, if it applies to the main clause. The period or the comma is always placed before the quotation mark (note example in 513); the colon or semicolon is placed outside:

"Are you ill?" she asked.

Did Father say, "Wait until tomorrow"?

Tom said, "Don't wait for me"; then he turned and walked away.

"The music was beautiful," she remarked.

If both the main clause of the sentence and the quotation are interrogative, only one question mark (529) is required:

Did Fred ask, "Where have you been?"

515 When a quotation is interrupted, an extra set of marks must be used:

"Come," he said, "as soon as you have the time."

516 There is often an erroneous impression among students that all inter-
ruptions of quotations are marked by commas. Use the sentence
marks which should be used regardless of the quotation:

> "You have delayed too long already," he said. "Success comes to people
> who act."
>
> "I am sure!" she exclaimed; "there is no doubt about it."

Apostrophe

517 Use the apostrophe to indicate the omission of letters from words. It
should be placed immediately above the point of omission:

> The man *isn't* here.
>
> Do not confuse: *its* for *it's*; *your* for *you're*; *where* for *where'er*.

518 The apostrophe may be used with s to denote plurals of letters, figures, signs, symbols, and words considered merely as words (88):

> She used two *a's*, three *b's*, two 8*'s* (or 8s), two *and's* (or *ands*).

519 The apostrophe is used in forming the possessive of nouns and indefinite pronouns. To form the possessive singular, add the apostrophe
and s (120):

> The *bird's* plumage is brilliant.
>
> He is *everyone's* friend.

> To form the possessive plural of a noun whose plural ends in s,
> add an apostrophe only (121):

> *Boys'* suits are on sale.

> ♦ Some Greek names, some Biblical names, and a few words (120)
> are traditional exceptions to the general rules:

> Euripides' tragedies   Moses' laws   conscience' sake

520 The possessives of the personal pronouns such as *its, his, hers, ours,*
yours, and *theirs* (146) do not use the apostrophe. But indefinite pronouns, such as *either, one,* and *other,* do use the apostrophe:

> The cat wants *its* (not *it's*) dinner. (*Its* is **possessive**.)
>
> *It's* time to go home. (*It's* is a **contraction**, 146, 517.)
>
> One must do *one's* duty, but always respect the *other's* rights.

521 The apostrophe is sometimes omitted in geographic names, organization names, or company names, in which the idea of possession seems
self-evident:

> Pikes Peak, Citizens National Bank, Teachers College

Dash

522 A dash is used to mark a sudden change or break in a sentence:

The boy went there—where did he go?

"There is no—" The speaker could not go on. (No period is needed after a dash which breaks off a sentence.)

Smith told me—but don't mention this—that he was bankrupt.

523 The dash may be used to set off a parenthetic group, especially when the parenthetic expression contains commas:

His food—nuts, berries, small game—was adequate for survival.

524 The dash may be used before a summarizing statement:

He planned, he worked, he sacrificed—all these he did that he might succeed.

525 The dash may be used to lend emphasis:

For a thousand dollars—a mere thousand dollars—he betrayed his friend.

♦ A double-length dash may be used to indicate the omission of letters or words:

Have you seen Captain H——   No, but I have seen——.
lately?

Parentheses and Brackets

526 Parentheses may be used to enclose matter apart from the main thought:

If you come to see me (and I hope you do come), be sure to bring your camera.

Matter enclosed in parentheses within a sentence, even though it forms a complete declarative or imperative sentence, need not begin with a capital and need not end with a period. But if it is interrogative or exclamatory, it ends with the appropriate mark (529, 530, 531):

She says that you insulted her (did you?) and that she is furious.

527 The punctuation mark belonging to matter given before that set off by parentheses should be placed after the second parenthesis mark (see the first example sentence given in 526):

When you receive your appointment (and I hope you receive it soon), you must tell me of your plans.

When a complete, independent sentence is placed in parentheses, the final punctuation is placed inside the parentheses:

(These theories will be further explained in the next chapter.)

528 Brackets are used to enclose explanatory matter that one inserts in a quotation from another writer:

"It was this poem ['The Raven'] that made Poe famous."

Question Mark

529 Place a question mark after every direct question. Although the very short declarative sentence (25) within parentheses (486) does not require a period, the short interrogative sentence (27) so used must close with a question mark (526):

> Have you seen my new hat?
>
> When you come to see me (why not come soon?), I will tell you about my trip to Denver.

If the main clause of a sentence and the dependent clause are both interrogative (27), only one question mark (514) is used. No question mark is used after an indirect question. After a polite request a period should be used instead of a question mark:

> Did the coach ask, "When did you return?"
>
> He inquired what the trouble was.
>
> Will you please send the check at once.

530 A question mark within parentheses is used to express uncertainty about dates or other information:

> Lucretius, 96(?)–55 B.C.

In sentences it is usually better to use *about* or *probably* than to use the question mark; in this case: Lucretius was born *about* 96 B.C.

Exclamation Mark

531 The exclamation mark is used after words, expressions, or sentences to show strong feeling or forceful utterance:

> Fire! Fire!   How terrible it was!

An exclamation within parentheses (526) retains the exclamation mark:

> She left the door unlocked (how thoughtless!) and drove to the store.

Hyphenation

532 A hyphen should be used to join words combined into a single adjective modifier: *well-to-do, self-supporting, far-flung.*

Adverbs ending in *ly* do not change into hyphened compound modifiers: a *beautifully illustrated* story.

533 The hyphen is omitted when certain compound modifiers follow the word modified and a linking verb, but true compounds retain the hyphen in this position:

> His mother is self-supporting.   His mother is well liked.

Use your dictionary as a guide to the correct usage of compounds.

534 Hyphens are used in spelling compound numbers from twenty-one to ninety-nine.

535 Fractions are hyphenated only when used as modifiers:

> One half of the book is finished. (**noun**)
> The box is two-thirds full. (**adverb**)
> He won by a two-thirds majority. (**adjective**)

536 A **compound word** is one that is made up of two or more words. Sometimes the words are joined together either with or without a hyphen. The purpose of a compound is to express an idea that the component parts do not express separately, either in meaning or in grammatical function. The use of a hyphen in a compound word may help a reader to avoid misreading confusing letter combinations and to make a visual distinction for proper word stress. Examples:

> 1. *red coat* (garment); 2. *redcoat* (soldier); 3. *red-coated* (covered with red).

A good dictionary is the best guide to the correct form to use: separate words or words joined with or without a hyphen.

537 When it is necessary to divide a word at the end of a line, the division should be made between syllables, and a hyphen should be placed at the end of the line. Never place a hyphen at the beginning of a line. Always check the dictionary for correct syllabication of English words.

Abbreviations and Contractions

538 The following rules should be observed in using abbreviations and contractions (see also 487):

1. The use of many abbreviations in formal writing indicates carelessness on the part of the writer. However, there are a few abbreviations which are used regularly in formal writing: A.D., B.C., A.M., P.M., (when used with figures); Mr., Mrs., Ms., Dr. (when used with names).

2. It is considered impolite to abbreviate titles such as the following when used before the last name only: *Captain, General, Colonel, Professor, President.*

3. The old rule was to place a period after each abbreviation, but there are a growing number of exceptions to the rule (see 487).

> Contractions and Roman numerals used in sentences do not require periods after them:

> He doesn't live here.   James II was king of England.

> Periods are not used with scientific or technical symbols: H_2SO_4, sin, tan, cos.

> Always refer to a dictionary for unfamiliar forms.

Italics (Underlining)

539 The following rules should be observed in using italics:

1. In writing in longhand and in typing, place one line under a word to indicate that it should be printed in italics.

2. Italicize foreign terms which have not become anglicized. A dictionary is the only safe guide in determining these words.

3. Italicize a word, phrase, or letter used as a subject of discussion (see also 508):

The word *receive* is often misspelled.

4. Use italics to indicate the titles of books, magazines, newspapers and the names of ships, named trains, aircraft, and man-made space-craft:

We have just read *The Sea Around Us* by Rachel L. Carson and an article, "Pollution of the Air," in *Harper's*.

On February 20, 1962, John H. Glenn, Jr., made three orbits of the earth in *Friendship 7*. *Apollo 15*, with astronauts Scott, Irvin, and Worden, began its famous trip to the moon on July 26, 1971.

5. In current usage, an article (285, 287) used in the title of a magazine or newspaper need not be italicized. The name of a city is not italicized if it is not an actual part of a journal's name. Although *magazine* is often used along with a title to make an identification of a journal clear, the word is not italicized with the name:

We read the Chicago *Sun-Times* and *Natural History* magazine.

6. It is permissible to italicize a word for emphasis, but this use of italics should be rare:

He *would* go back in spite of everything.

Numerals

540 The following rules should be observed in writing numerals:

1. Dates, street numbers, page numbers, decimals, and percents should be written in figures:

Columbus reached the New World on *October 12, 1492*.

Tom lives at 16 Spruce Street.   His address is listed on page 16.

Jim got 60 percent of the vote for class president.

2. The sign $ is not used for a sum less than one dollar:

The knife cost 65¢.

3. The general rule for writing numbers is to spell out a number if it may be done in one or two words; otherwise, it should be written in figures:

He gave me *one thousand* dollars.   I ate one-third of a pie.

She gave me 1,397 copies of the paper; there were 10,491 printed.

4. When several numbers (used as statistics) are mentioned within a short space of text, use figures for all.

5. A number that represents a person's age or one denoting the hour of the day is usually spelled out:

At *three o'clock* there is to be a meeting of the students who are between *sixteen* and *eighteen* years of age.

6. Do not begin a sentence with figures:

Six hundred twenty-five (not 625) students were at the meeting.

7. It is not necessary, except in special instances such as contracts or laws, to place numerals in parentheses after written numbers; but when they are used, each should follow the number it repeats:

I am sending you *fifteen* (15) *bushels* of wheat.

8. In technical, mathematical, and business writing, figures are generally used:

125 square feet, $6.00 a pound, 4½ percent, 9.6 meters.

5

The Paragraph

Think of the house you live in as if it were a composition. Everything about your house has a specific name and function—the words of language. Each window or door, every wall or roof, is related to the whole—words in proper combination become the sentence. Each room, with its doors, windows, walls, ceiling, and furniture, becomes a unit of the whole—the sentences in logical sequence become the paragraph. Your house is made up of a series of rooms (unless it is a one-room house!)—the paragraphs in their turn become a composition. Compositions, like the houses people live in, have many styles: essay, story, letter, news report, speech, research paper, sermon, poem, novel, play, review, précis.

Structure and Analysis

541 **WHAT IS A PARAGRAPH?**   The paragraph is usually described as a group of sentences developing a single topic. Sometimes a paragraph may consist of a single topic sentence; at other times, several paragraphs may be needed to develop a topic.

542 **LENGTH OF THE PARAGRAPH**   The length of the paragraph in general writing is determined primarily by the extent to which the ideas are developed. This rule, however, is not arbitrary and may be modified, as for instance in the business letter (589.11), in which the short paragraph is more effective than the longer one. In dialogue, of course, each speech is separately paragraphed, as a rule.

543 PARAGRAPH SENSE Every good writer develops a paragraph sense, just as he develops a sentence sense (36). This sense may be acquired by thinking in terms of topics and by adhering strictly to each topic under discussion.

544 TOPIC SENTENCE The sentence that presents the topic to be discussed is called the **topic sentence**. It is often stated at the beginning of the paragraph—but it may occur at any point in a paragraph—and its position may be varied to avoid monotony. The paragraph following, from Emerson's "Compensation," illustrates the beginning topic sentence:

> *A man cannot speak but he judges himself.* With his will or against his will he draws his portrait to the eye of his companions by every word. Every opinion reacts on him who utters it. It is a threadball thrown at a mark, but the other end remains in the thrower's bag. Or rather, it is a harpoon thrown at the whale, unwinding, as it flies, a coil of cord in the boat, and, if the harpoon is not good, or not well thrown, it will go nigh to cut the steersman in twain or to sink the boat.

♦ Often no one sentence expresses the topic. But make sure that, except for transition paragraphs, a topic can be identified for each paragraph.

545 DEVELOPING THE TOPIC There are many ways of developing the topic, some of the most common being the use of *details, examples, comparison* or *contrast, reasons,* or a combination of any two or more of these methods. An illustration is given for each of the first three and for a paragraph describing a process:

1. **Details.** Giving details makes a topic more vivid and develops at greater length what is suggested in the topic. Here is a familiar paragraph from "The Legend of Sleepy Hollow," by Washington Irving.

> All was now bustle and hubbub in the late quiet schoolroom. The scholars were hurried through their lessons, without stopping at trifles; those who were nimble skipped over half with impunity, and those who were tardy had a smart application now and then in the rear, to quicken their speed, or help them over a tall word. Books were flung aside without being put away on the shelves, inkstands were overturned, benches thrown down, and the whole school was turned loose an hour before the usual time, bursting forth like a legion of young imps, yelping and racketing about the green, in joy of their early emancipation.

2. **Examples.** Concrete examples are given to illustrate the general suggestion of the topic:

Riverside Park is noted for the beauty and variety of its native trees. Along the river to the south are many excellent specimens of elm, sycamore, cottonwood, and hackberry. To the west, covering several acres, is a grove of tall, beautiful black walnut trees, shading here and there a less stately mulberry. To the north the park abounds in large shapely oaks, some of which thrust out protecting arms above clumps of timid redbuds. Other less prominent specimens scattered throughout the park are ash, box elder, and Osage orange.

3. **Contrast.** Through contrast, differences are made to stand out more prominently. Notice the effect of this method in this excerpt from *Adam Bede,* a novel by George Eliot:

It is clear at a glance that the next workman is Adam's brother. He is nearly as tall; he has the same type of features, the same hue of hair and complexion; but the strength of the family likeness seems only to render more conspicuous the remarkable difference of expression both in form and face. Seth's broad shoulders have a slight stoop; his eyes are grey; his eyebrows have less prominence and more repose than his brother's; and his glance, instead of being keen, is confiding and benign. . . .

In developing a topic explaining a process, such as telling how to do something or how something works, follow the normal order through different stages, or give a step-by-step sequence.

When you speak, your vocal chords vibrate. The vibrations cause changes in the pressure of the air. Waves of sound are set up. When the sound waves reach another person, they strike the eardrum. The eardrum vibrates according to the changing pressure of the air on it. The person hears.

546 MECHANICS OF WRITING PARAGRAPHS

1. Indent the first line of each paragraph. In longhand, it is customary to indent about an inch; in typing, the usual indentation is five or ten spaces.

2. Do not leave a part of a line blank except at the close of the paragraph.

3. Except in dialogue, where paragraph length is arbitrary, paragraphs should seldom be made either extremely long or short.

4. In dialogue, begin a paragraph with each change of speaker.

5. Keep the left margin of the paragraph uniform and the right margin reasonably so. Paragraph indention should be uniform.

6. Make the transition from paragraph to paragraph easy and natural, sometimes by the use of appropriate transition words (549), but always by proper arrangement.

♦ Some business firms do not indent typewritten paragraphs in their letters. This style is called **flush-paragraphing**, or **block style**. Sometimes, too, printers begin paragraphs at the margin as an element of the typographic design.

Paragraph Requirements

547 The paragraph, like the sentence (433–435), must have **unity, coherence**, and **emphasis**.

548 **Unity in the paragraph** is attained when every sentence bears directly upon the topic of that particular paragraph. Any departure from the central topic means that a new paragraph should be formed. In the following paragraph the italicized sentence is irrelevant and therefore should be eliminated:

> Home computers will revolutionize the way we learn, shop, conduct business, and even entertain ourselves. A home computer can help you with your math homework, retrieve information from the library for your book report, or show you what to do in a medical emergency. For relaxation, a computer can be an ideal chess partner, or it can provide hours of "Star Wars" video games for you and your friends. *The computer is very expensive to fix if it breaks down.* With these and many other functions, a home computer will be a worthwhile, perhaps a necessary, investment in the near future.

549 **Coherence in the paragraph** results from the correct arrangement of the parts of a paragraph—an arrangement in which each part of the paragraph is often aided by the use of appropriate transitional words, but too many such words results in a heavy, stilted style. Careful arrangement is the important means of attaining coherence. Transition words are so numerous that one such word may be found to suit the exact need of almost any transition.

Transition words are used to show: (a) passing of time; (b) addition; (c) contrast or opposition; (d) comparison and similarity; (e) concession, admission of facts; (f) sequence or numerical order; (g) result; (h) summary.

Some of the more commonly used of these words and phrases are *furthermore, however, for this reason, consequently, in addition, not-withstanding, all things considered, to this end, hence, above all, for example, as a consequence, on the contrary, nevertheless, as a result, but, otherwise, yet, still, meanwhile, presently, finally, in conclusion, for instance, therefore, and accordingly.*

The paragraph below illustrates the smooth use of transition words. In order to see the importance of arrangement, try placing the next-to-the-last sentence as the concluding sentence. This will show the loss in force of the paragraph that is not coherent:

> Barbara had given up a lot to prepare for the tennis championship. She practiced for two hours after school every day. As a result, she had to take time off from her job at the record shop. Her coach told her to get plenty of rest the week before the match. Consequently, she told all her friends not to call after 9 p.m. Between practice and schoolwork, she had little time for her social life. But now, the day of the match was here and it was pouring. Temporarily, at least, sports seemed to Barbara not worth the trouble.

550 Emphasis in the paragraph results from giving stress to the important ideas. If more space is given to the important ideas than to the unimportant, there is the possibility of interfering with unity and coherence; therefore, it may be best to give emphasis by position. The beginning or the close of the paragraph is the most emphatic position. The paragraph below from "The Masque of the Red Death," a short story by Poe, is a good illustration of proper emphasis in the paragraph. Note how shifting of the last sentence to the middle of the paragraph would weaken the entire effect:

> And now was acknowledged the presence of the Red Death. He had come like a thief in the night. And one by one dropped the revelers in the blood-bedewed halls of their revel, and each died in the despairing posture of his fall. And the life of the ebony clock went out with that of the last of the gay. And the flames of the tripods expired. And Darkness and Decay and the Red Death held illimitable dominion over all.

Forms of Discourse

551 There are four types of expression, known as **forms of discourse,** and every paragraph illustrates one of these types or a combination of two or more of them. These four forms are **exposition, description, narration, argumentation.**

Exposition

552 **Exposition** is explaining, or giving information about, something. Of

all the forms of discourse, it is the one most commonly used. Expository writing may be approached in several ways:

1. **Defining:** Explaining what something is or what its purpose or function may be.

2. **Classifying:** Explaining what something is by identifying its type or by fitting it into the larger scheme of which it is a part.

3. **Analyzing:** Explaining what something is by outlining its constituent parts and showing how they are organized or by placing it in its historical or strategic context.

Use details, examples, comparison and contrast, and reasons to help support statements of general ideas.

> Comets orbit the sun, but their orbits are not like those of the planets. The orbits of comets are highly eccentric. A comet may come as close to the sun as a million kilometers, then zoom into space as far out as thousands of millions of kilometers. Not even Pluto's eccentric orbit can approach the oddity of a comet's path. Further, the orbits of comets are inclined in many directions, but they never fall into the same plane as those of the planets in the Solar System. Comets have so little mass that they cannot affect the orbits of planetary bodies, but Jupiter and Saturn have attracted comets that ventured too near. These planets are known to have changed the orbits of several cometary bodies in space.

Description

553 **Description** is picturing in words. Pure description is seldom met with in discourse, for it needs the other forms to give it movement. It is made vivid by the use of meaningful words, particularly adjectives (275) and nouns (39). The paragraph given below, from Mark Twain's *Roughing It*, is a good illustration of description. Note the descriptive words *memorable, bottomless, dreary, long, thirsty, white with bones, prodigious, rotting.*

> On the nineteenth day we crossed the Great American Desert— forty memorable miles of bottomless sand, into which the coach wheels sunk from six inches to a foot. We worked our passage most of the way across. That is to say, we got out and walked. It was a dreary pull and a long and thirsty one, for we had no water. From one extremity of this desert to the other, the road was white with the bones of oxen and horses. It would hardly be an exaggeration to say that we could have walked the forty miles and set our feet on a bone at every step. The desert was one prodigious graveyard. And the log-chains, wagon tires, and rotting wrecks of vehicles were almost as thick as the bones. I think we saw log-chains enough rusting there in the desert to reach across any state in the Union.

Narration

554 **Narration** is the telling of a story, whether the story is truth or fiction. This may be done best by the selection of events that are essential to the story, by the proper use of transitional expressions that show: (a) continuation of thought; (b) passing of time; (c) result; (d) opposition. Narration is often associated with exposition and description, and it must give the effect of movement from event to event. The many stories with which we are familiar are examples of narration. Those who write or tell stories should observe these precautions for successful narration: **Make** a prompt, effective beginning; **stick** to the story; **tell** the story simply; **end** it promptly.

Point of view is of key importance in narration. First-person point of view (*I*) and third-person point of view (*he, she, they*) indicate, respectively, that the teller is an actor in the story or that the teller is an observer of a story about others. Consistency in the use of verb tenses and transitional words is essential since they differ for the two points of view.

Argumentation

555 **Argumentation** is an effort to show by logical arrangement of facts that a statement is true or false, as in a mathematical demonstration such as the proof of a proposition in geometry. When one attempts to establish a new conviction in written matter, one explains facts favorable to that conviction: this is argumentation. To be successful in argumentation, one must exercise the same tact and skills as in the other forms. Much good may be achieved through written argumentation, but in the verbal contacts of everyday life, tact must be applied.

Development of Creative Expression

556 **Creative expression** is the communication of a feeling or experience that is worth sharing with others just for its own sake. This is the type of expression which at its best gives us our literature. But all of us, whether or not we have the urge or the genius to become great creative artists, should give thought to creative expression, since it may help us to observe more closely the things about us. We become more critical of ourselves and others and thus better able to analyze our own behavior and to be more sympathetic with the behavior of others. Through this type of expression we may eventually have a broader understanding of life and its problems.

Précis–Writing

557 Ability to Condense Expression It is important that one should learn how to condense one's meaning into the fewest possible words. The ability to condense the expression of others to the fewest possible words should also be acquired. Such a condensed form of expression retains the thought and emphasis of the original and is called a précis.

558 The Précis A standard definition of the précis is a "brief summary of essential points, statements, or facts." It differs from a **paraphrase** in that it is much shorter and more precisely and accurately written. It must retain in few words the ideas of the original, and these ideas must be clearly and forcefully expressed. The length of the précis may vary with the intensity of the thought, but a good general average would be to reduce the number of words to one third or one fourth the original. The writer of the précis must grasp the entire meaning of the expression to be condensed (562).

559 Suggestions for Précis–Writing Précis-writing is excellent exercise for inexperienced writers who have a tendency to wordiness (462). Here are some general suggestions:

1. Be sure you understand what you are trying to condense.
2. Follow the original without changing the order of the thought.
3. Use your own words.
4. Write as clearly and forcefully as possible.

560 Illustration Below is an illustration of précis-writing in which each of five summaries of a paragraph is rated by expert authority. The test paragraph, given first, is followed by instructions for grading and five summaries. (The extract is "Selection V, Form A" from the *Poley Précis Test*, a standard test by Irwin C. Poley, Public School Publishing Company, Bloomington, Illinois. Reprinted by permission of the publisher.)

> Vandalism in the parks is all too typical of one side of the American character. We seem incapable of bearing in mind an idea of decency in the abstract. As guests, if our host is a friend, we treat him with courtesy; but if he is unknown and not at hand to watch us we concede him no rights whatever; as hunters borrowing somebody's land we drop cigarettes and start forest fires; as campers borrowing somebody's woods we have a litter of cans and refuse that is notorious. . . . We are callous to the idea that things ought not to be destroyed, no matter who owns them or who will use them. . . . Park vandals are guests of the public, and they should have enough regard for the host not to destroy his property. They use the parks in common with many other people and they should have a thought to the comfort of others.

> Editorial, New York *World*

INSTRUCTIONS: Below are five summaries of the paragraph just given. Try to rate the summaries as to accuracy and completeness. The ratings as given by the author of the test appear after the last summary.

a. Americans are apt to be discourteous in their treatment of public parks. They should remember that consideration is due as much to an absent or public host as to a present or private one.

b. In America the parks are littered with trash, especially cigarettes, which may start a forest fire. Private property should be respected as much as public.

c. Private property should be respected as much as public property, if not more. Parks are sure to be littered with refuse, and public camping sites are spoiled.

d. If hunters borrow land, they should be careful not to drop cigarettes and thus start a fire. Campers should not leave a litter of refuse behind them; even if they do not know the owner, they should be considerate of the property.

e. Americans should learn to get along pleasantly with people they meet in the park. The public is our host, and individuals should try to act as courteously to one another as they do in Europe.

The five summaries are rated as follows: a best expresses the thought of the original paragraph; b, c, and e are inaccurate (that is, they contain actual errors of statement); d is inadequate (that is, it misses the central thought of the original paragraph although it contains no error of statement).

Critical Reading

561 READING "There is an art of reading, as well as an art of thinking, and an art of writing." This aphorism by Isaac D'Israeli, written in 1791, is still as valid as when it was written. Critical reading has the major task of grasping the thought of the writer; a secondary task is observing the mechanical techniques used in expressing it. These techniques include the spelling, grammar, punctuation, and capitalization employed in writing down the thoughts. A reading of this kind is referred to as proofreading.

562 READING FOR THOUGHT Reading for content may be done for a number of reasons. One may read the newspapers as a daily habit for the current events reported there. Or one may read magazines and books from a desire to learn about the opinions and experiences of others or to enlarge personal horizons.

A more serious purpose of the reader may be to gather material for a paper or a speech through extensive reading in a library. The reader usually accompanies this type of reading with note-taking, the purpose of which is to gather facts.

Every reader should learn to grasp and quickly pinpoint the main ideas while reading. The principal facts in a newspaper article may be learned by reading the headlines and lead paragraphs. One should train oneself to glean from every paragraph the necessary facts by writing brief, clear notes or a précis (557). Accurate reading and expert précis-writing go hand in hand, both being invaluable aids to anyone who wishes to attain effective expression.

563 **PROOFREADING** In addition to learning to get the thought from written expression, one must learn to detect mechanical errors in it. Reading for the purpose of correcting mechanical errors is called **proofreading**, though in the strictest sense this term is applied only to the correction of proof sheets for a printer. You may use any simple system of marking errors in proofreading your own work or the work of others. Appropriate rules for correcting such errors are to be found in the various sections of this book. Those interested in reading real printer's proof will find a list of standard symbols in *Webster's Ninth New Collegiate Dictionary*, page 943.

Writing Verse

564 **EXPRESSION IN VERSE** Verse is a form of composition that is very different from prose. It is so constructed that it has rhythm—rhythm is heard by the ear and not seen by the eye—and this rhythm is generally produced by a regular arrangement of stressed and unstressed syllables.

The writing of verse is a satisfying creative expression and good practice in acquiring skill in the use of words. In addition, the writing of light or humorous verse may be entertaining. It gives variety to expression that, in prose, has a tendency to become sedate. The next few sections explain the structure of verse.

565 **VERSE FORMS** Before one attempts to write verse, one should become familiar with the simple mechanics of versification given here.

1. **Verse.** The term *verse* may be applied (by a figure of speech called *synecdoche*, the substitution of the name of a part for the whole, 682) to rhythmical composition in general, but in a more restricted sense it indicates a line of verse. A verse, then, of poetry is one line, not a group of lines.

2. **Stanza.** A stanza is a group of lines (verses) bound together by some rhyme scheme (570) which is usually repeated in the poem.

3. **Foot.** A foot is simply a unit of measurement of the rhythm of a verse and consists of accented and unaccented syllables.

4. **Kinds of Feet.** There are four kinds of feet in popular use, though there are others less often used. The four are **iambic, trochaic, anapaestic,** and **dactylic.**

   a. **Iambic.** The iambic foot consists of one *unaccented* syllable followed by one *accented:* ex-PEL.

   b. **Trochaic.** A trochaic foot is made up of one *accented* syllable followed by one *unaccented:* BEAU-ty.

   c. **Anapaestic.** An anapaestic foot has two *unaccented* syllables followed by one *accented:* in-ter-VENE.

   d. **Dactylic.** A dactylic foot has one *accented* syllable followed by two *unaccented:* BEAU-ti-ful.

5. **Number of Feet in a Line.** A line (verse) is classified by the number of feet it contains. A line of one foot is called a **monometer;** two feet, **dimeter;** three feet, **trimeter;** four feet, **tetrameter;** five feet, **pentameter;** six feet, **hexameter;** seven feet, **heptameter;** and eight feet, **octameter.**

566 **THE NAME OF THE LINE**   A line gets its name from the number and kind of feet it contains. For example, a line of five iambic feet is called **iambic pentameter.** Here are illustrations taken from familiar poems:

   (iambic tetrameter) I think | that I | shall nev- | er see. ("Trees")

   (trochaic tetrameter) Téll me | nót in | móurn-ful | núm-bers.
                                                            ("A Psalm of Life")

   (anapaestic tetrameter) For the móon | nev-er béams | with-out bring- | ing me dréams.   ("Annabel Lee")

   (dactylic hexameter) Bláck were her | eýes as the | bér-ry that | gróws on the | thórn by the | wáy-side.   ("Evangeline")

567 **RHYME**   Rhyme is correspondence, in two or more words, of ending sounds beginning with the last accented vowel. The preceding consonant sounds should be different, though rhymes are not always perfect:

   Rhymes: relate, sedate; willing, fulfilling

   Imperfect rhymes: relate, elate; imply, reply

568 **RHYTHM**   Verse rhythm is the regular recurrence of accented and unaccented syllables. Rhythm is necessary to verse, but the use of rhyme is not. Verse with regular rhythm but without rhyme is called blank verse. Another kind of verse without rhyme is called free verse. It has rhythmical cadence, but does not depend on a strict arrangement of the accented and unaccented syllables.

569 BLANK VERSE Any unrhymed verse may be called blank verse, but this term is applied especially to iambic pentameter, the kind of verse used in Shakespeare's plays.

570 RHYME SCHEME A stanza usually has a regular rhyme scheme. That is, each stanza in a given poem has corresponding lines that rhyme with each other. Rhyme scheme is represented by letters of the alphabet; a first rhyme is represented by *a*, a second by *b*, and so on.

571 STANZA FORMS Some of the stanza forms much used are the **sonnet** (572–574), the **limerick** (576), and the **quatrain**. The example of the quatrain given below is from MacLeish's "You, Andrew Marvel." It is made up of four iambic tetrameter lines (566) rhyming alternately (*a, b, a, b*):

> And here face down beneath the sun
> And here upon earth's noonward height
> To feel the always coming on
> The always rising of the night:

572 SONNET The sonnet is a form that has long been popular. It consists of fourteen iambic pentameter lines with a strict rhyme scheme. There are two well-known forms, the **Italian**, or **Petrarchan**, sonnet, and the **English**, or **Shakespearean**, sonnet.

573 ITALIAN SONNET The Italian sonnet has the more rigid rhyme scheme, which demands but two rhymes in the first eight lines (octave) and restricts the rhyming of the last six lines (sestet). The rhyme of the octave is *a b b a a b b a*. The sestet may vary its rhyme scheme, though the last two lines should not rhyme together. This example of the Italian sonnet is by the English lyric poet, John Keats:

> ON THE GRASSHOPPER AND CRICKET
>
> The po | etry | of earth | is ne | ver dead: *a*
> When all the birds are faint with the hot sun,   *b*
> And hide in cooling trees, a voice will run   *b*
> From hedge to hedge about the new-mown mead;   *a*
> That is the Grasshopper's—he takes the lead   *a*
> In summer luxury,—he has never done   *b*
> With his delights; for when tired out with fun   *b*
> He rests at ease beneath some pleasant weed.   *a*
> The poetry of earth is ceasing never: *c*
> On a lone winter evening, when the frost   *d*
> Has wrought a silence, from the stove there shrills   *e*
> The Cricket's song, in warmth increasing ever,   *c*
> And seems to one in drowsiness half lost,   *d*
> The grasshopper's among some grassy hills.   *e*

574 ENGLISH SONNET The English, or Shakespearean, sonnet is made up of three quatrains with alternate rhyme and a rhyming couplet. The rhyme scheme used by Shakespeare is *a b a b/c d c d/e f e f/g g*. One of Shakespeare's sonnets is given here:

> SONNET LXIV
>
> When I | have seen | by Time's | fell hand | defaced   *a*
> The rich proud cost of outworn buried age;   *b*
> When sometime lofty towers I see down-razed   *a*
> And brass eternal slave to mortal rage;   *b*
> When I have seen the hungry ocean gain   *c*
> Advantage on the kingdom of the shore,   *d*
> And the firm soil win of the watery main,   *c*
> Increasing store with loss and loss with store;   *d*
> When I have seen such interchange of state,   *e*
> Or state itself confounded in decay;   *f*
> Ruin hath taught me thus to ruminate,   *e*
> That Time will come and take my love away.   *f*
> This thought is as a death, which cannot choose   *g*
> But weep to have that which it fears to lose.   *g*

575 TYPES OF VERSE There are many types of verse ranging from nonsense rhymes to the most exalted poetry. Only the types of verse expressing emotion as well as idea should be called poetry. The limerick below is a good example of light verse; the two sonnets (573, 574) are classed as poetry.

576 LIGHT VERSE Light or humorous verse may be written on a variety of subjects or in imitation of familiar poems or songs. A bit of writing in imitation of another is called a **parody**. The example of light verse below is in limerick form. The first, second, and fifth rhyming lines of the limerick are roughly anapaestic trimeter (565). The third and fourth lines are anapaestic dimeter rhyming together. Any line of a limerick may begin with either one or two unaccented syllables. This limerick by an anonymous poet contains lines of both types:

> A SIGHTSEER NAMED SUE
>
> There was a sightseer named Sue
> Who saw a strange beast at the zoo.
>   When she asked, "Is it old?"
>   She was smilingly told,
> "It's not an old beast, but a gnu."

The Whole Composition

I keep six honest serving men
(They taught me all I know);
Their names are *What* and *Why* and *When*
And *How* and *Where* and *Who*.
RUDYARD KIPLING, *Just So Stories* (1902)

Planning the Composition

577 THE COMPARISON AS A UNIT   Not only should your sentences and paragraphs maintain unity, coherence, and emphasis but the composition as a whole should also maintain these three qualities. The composition must be a unit with its parts arranged to show their relationship clearly. In addition, the most important ideas must be in those positions that give them the greatest emphasis—the beginning and the close.

578 ORGANIZING MATERIAL   A simple plan for news stories may be made by answering the questions: *Who? When? Where? What? Why?*
   Who—Our club
   When—Next Thursday
   Where—Glenwood Park
   What—A picnic
   Why—To entertain our new members
   Another excellent general plan for organizing material for a composition is to jot down all thoughts on the subject as they occur, at first

115

with no attempt at orderly arrangement, and then later to assemble the ideas in related groups as a complete outline. The topics in such an outline should be arranged in their logical order, somewhat as they are arranged in the outline below:

MARKET GARDENING

1. *Deciding* what to plant
2. *Selecting* the seed
3. *Preparing* the soil
4. *Planting* the seed
5. *Cultivating* the growing plants
6. *Gathering* the produce
7. *Preparing* the produce for market
8. *Selling* the produce

579 TOPIC OUTLINE A topic outline is made up of headings that indicate the main ideas for the composition. Terms of the same rank should be parallel. For example, the main headings in the outline below are all nouns: Pleasure, Health, Citizenship:

TENNIS IS A GOOD GAME FOR STUDENTS

I. Pleasure
   A. Relaxation from study
   B. Enjoyment of competition
II. Health
   A. Stimulation of bodily functions
   B. Increase in mental alertness
III. Citizenship
   A. Development of cooperation
   B. Development of regard for others

580 SENTENCE OUTLINES The sentence outline has complete sentences:

TENNIS IS A GOOD GAME FOR STUDENTS

I. It provides pleasure.
   A. The change from study to play relieves tension.
   B. The thrill of competition is stimulating.
II. It promotes health.
   A. The outdoor exercise is good for the body.
   B. The keen interest in the game keeps the brain alert.
III. It develops good citizenship.
   A. The contact with others discourages selfishness.
   B. The rules of the game make necessary a regard for the rights of others.

♦ The **paragraph outline** is made by expanding the material into complete paragraphs. It is not so frequently used as are the two forms given—topic and sentence.

581 NUMBERING THE ELABORATE OUTLINE The subscripts are properly labeled this way: I., A., 1., 2., 3. . . . , a., b., c. . . . , (1), (2), (3), . . . , (a), (b), (c), . . . ; I., B., 1., . . . , a., . . . , (1) . . . , (a) . . . ; II., A., 1., . . . , a., . . . , (1), . . . , (a), . . . ; II., B., 1. . . . , etc.

Written Composition

582 There are two general classes of composition—**oral** and **written**. Written composition will be discussed first.

583 **Written composition** includes every form of writing. This brief outline may give some idea of its great variety and importance.

584 TYPES OF WRITTEN COMPOSITION Of the many types of written composition, the following are some of the most familiar: fiction, history, biography, essay, poetry, newspaper reporting, and the letter. Because the letter is the type of composition most widely used by people in general, it is discussed in detail.

585 LETTERS Comparatively few people become professional writers, but everyone has occasion to write letters. The successful businessperson must write letters of professional quality, and everyone must at times write letters of personal importance.

586 CLASSES OF LETTERS There are only two general classes of letters—business and social. The business letter includes all forms written for business purposes. The social letter varies from the informal letter of friendship to the most formal note. A letter, of course, may be a combination of the two classes.

Business Correspondence

587 BUSINESS LETTERS The writing of business letters is not confined to people who are in business. Practically every person has occasion to write about transactions not related to the social affairs of life.

588 IMPORTANCE OF THE BUSINESS LETTER A great part of the world's business is transacted through exchange of letters; therefore, the business letter is of tremendous importance. The very difficult art of business letter writing is challenging the finest talent in the world of commerce today.

589 REQUIREMENTS OF A GOOD BUSINESS LETTER Requirements of a good business letter are the following: promptness, accuracy, clarity,

economy, completeness, correctness, courtesy, neatness, friendliness, effective sentence construction, proper paragraphing, proper diction and correct spelling, and freedom from hackneyed expressions. Each of these is worthy of short comment:

1. **Promptness.** A business letter should be answered at once.

2. **Accuracy.** A letter that is not accurate in form or in content implies that the writer is either careless or lacking in ability to communicate.

3. **Clearness.** One of the first essentials of a business letter is clarity. Weak sentences (437–449) may cause confusion of meaning.

4. **Economy.** A letter should be so written that every word serves a distinct purpose. It should be as brief as is consistent with clearness and courtesy, but all sentences should be complete.

5. **Completeness.** A business letter should be so complete in itself as to make unnecessary any further correspondence to supplement it.

6. **Correctness.** No letter can be strong enough in other ways to overcome the handicap of incorrect language or form.

7. **Courtesy.** A letter lacking in courtesy reflects discredit on the writer and on the business he or she represents. An effective means of showing courtesy is by stressing the *you* rather than the *I*.

8. **Neatness.** Neatness depends on the paper, margins, spacing, and typing. The paper is usually 8½ by 11 inches, of good quality, white in color, with envelopes to match. (Business letters should never be written on stationery meant for social letters.) Margins should be so spaced that they are in correct proportion to the letter, and the typed space should appear as a picture correctly set in a frame. Usually single spacing is used except between paragraphs and parts of the letter, where spacing is double. The typing should be clear and free from untidy, obvious erasures.

9. **Friendliness.** Effective business letters are those that have a friendly tone.

10. **Effective Sentence Construction.** Make all sentences effective (433–436). See that they are free from weaknesses of structure and style (438–457) and that they are varied (421–431).

11. **Proper Paragraphing.** The correct paragraphing of a business letter aids much in making its meaning clear. Long paragraphs are not so clear as shorter ones. Most writers of business letters prefer paragraphs of not more than six or eight lines. Proper arrangement of paragraphs is also vital.

12. **Proper Diction and Correct Spelling.** Each word should be chosen to convey the exact meaning intended, and no word should ever be misspelled.

13. **Freedom from Hackneyed Expressions.** There are expressions in business correspondence that have become obsolete through overuse. No modern streamlined letter should be marred by even one of these relics. The following are a few of those that were once most frequently used: *and oblige, as per, at hand, beg to state, early date, enclosed herewith,*

esteemed favor, has come to hand, kind favor, please note, recent date, we thank you kindly, we would advise, your favor of, yours to hand.

590 **PARTS OF THE BUSINESS LETTER**   There are six main parts of a business letter: **heading, inside address, salutation, body, complimentary close, signature.** Other parts of the business letter that might be included are the initials placed at the left lower margin of a dictated letter to indicate the dictator and the typist, and the outside address (on the envelope). Each of these parts requires separate discussion.

591 **HEADING OF THE BUSINESS LETTER**   The heading is placed at the upper right-hand corner (of stationery that does not have a printed letter-head) and consists of the exact address of the writer and the date. Its length will determine the number of lines it requires, though it usually consists of three or four lines. The first line should give the smallest division, such as box number, name of building, or street and number; then comes the name of the city and the state, followed by the Zip Code number. The last line is the date.

A date that is stated in terms of the day, month, and year is correct in form, but this form is not as widely used in letter-writing (except in the government) as it is in record-keeping: 15 December 1987 (15 Dec 87).

You may abbreviate the name of the state, using preferably the United States Post Office abbreviations, but not of the city, and write the street number in figures. Today's writers do not abbreviate the name of the month in headings. Of course, where printed stationery is used, the letterhead includes all the heading except the date. The day of the month and the year are usually written in figures.

592 **FORM OF THE HEADING**   The heading may be either of the block type or the indented. In the block type each line begins exactly the same distance from the right and left margins; in the indented type each succeeding line is spaced uniformly to the right. Examples are given below. The block form is almost always used in typing; the indented form may be used when writing in longhand:

```
    1255 Walnut Street          1255 Walnut Street
    Denver, CO  80202           Denver, CO  80202
    December 15, 19--            December 15, 19--
```

593 **PUNCTUATION OF THE HEADING**   Almost no punctuation appears in the heading except for the comma between the names of the city and state and the comma between the numbers indicating the day and year in the date.

594 INSIDE ADDRESS The inside address should be placed at the left margin below the heading; and it should give the proper courtesy title and business title, if any, correct name, and complete address of the person for whom the letter is intended. The form should be the same as that of the heading.

```
Mr. Hugh J. Dunn, Sales Manager
Colonial Quilts and Coverlets, Inc.
4230 Main Street
Houston, TX  77002
```

595 SALUTATION The salutation is placed at the left margin two spaces below the inside address. The following are appropriate salutations in greeting an individual whose name is known: *Dear Mr.* _____, *Dear Mrs.* _____, *Dear Ms.* _____, *Dear Miss* _____. In letters addressed to a firm or to an individual whose name is not known, *Dear Sir or Madam* is the most common greeting.

There are special forms of address and salutation for high dignitaries of the Church and the State, and courtesy demands that they be followed exactly. *Webster's Ninth New Collegiate Dictionary*, under "Forms of Address," page 1556, gives a list of such forms.

596 CAPITALIZATION OF THE SALUTATION If the salutation consists of two words, both are capitalized; but in a salutation such as *My dear General Smith*, the *dear* is not capitalized.

597 PUNCTUATION OF THE SALUTATION The punctuation mark used after the salutation in a business letter is the colon (494). There is a present trend to add friendliness to the business letter; therefore, the comma, less formal than the colon, might be used after the salutation of the more informal business letter to a friend.

598 BODY The body of the letter is the message. It should conform to all rules of good writing (see 589). The sentences should be made effective (see 421–463). The paragraphs should be short and forceful (see 547–550). All words should be well chosen, and each should add something to the effectiveness of the letter. Be careful to avoid the worn-out expressions (see 589.13) that brand a letter as stilted. Make your letter a part of you—give it your personality.

The opening sentence is especially vital, for on its effectiveness may depend the impact of the entire message. The first sentence should be specific and should make some personal appeal to the reader. It should stress *you*, not *I*. It should never begin with any of the following meaningless references to the receipt of a letter: *Pursuant to your request of the fifth, Answering your letter of October 5, We beg to acknowledge receipt of your letter of June 4, We are in receipt of your letter of May 9, Your letter of recent date at hand, Acknowledging yours of recent date, Supplementing your letter of March 16, We have your letter of April 3, Replying to yours of August 12, Complying with your request of recent date, Referring to your favor of June 6.* Such expressions were once acceptable, but they are now in the scrap heap of clichés except in certain legal correspondence.

The closing sentence is also very important. It should leave the reader feeling that he or she has just made contact with a cordial, friendly person.

When a letter is more than a page in length, the name of the person addressed, the page number, and the date should be placed at the top of each additional page. The margins should be the same for all pages. Five lines or more should appear on the last page.

599 COMPLIMENTARY CLOSE The complimentary close should be consistent with the other parts of the letter. It should never be preceded by the participial expressions once so popular, such as *Thanking you for your favor, Hoping this will be satisfactory, Awaiting your reply.* The last sentence should be complete, and it should say something vital. The close needs no such out-dated expressions as *I am* or *I remain* as an introduction. End the message with a forceful, appropriate sentence; then begin the close about the center of the page two spaces below. The following are correct in business letters: *Yours truly, Very truly yours, Yours sincerely, Sincerely yours.* The first word only of the close is capitalized. The close is punctuated with a comma at the end.

600 SIGNATURE The signature is placed just below the close. Place the signature so that its first letter is below the first letter of the close. Usually the writer's name is also typed just beneath the longhand signature. Every letter should, of course, be signed legibly in ink. The signature of a letter sent out by a business organization may include the name and position of the writer. The following are examples:

Yours truly,

Ralph W. Estes

Ralph W. Estes
Director of Personnel

Sincerely,

Frances Wilson

(Miss) Francis Wilson
Sales Manager

In signing a business letter, a married woman or a widow uses her own name, such as *Ann Clarke Brown*, or *Ann C. Brown*, not her married social name, *Mrs. Frank R. Brown*. She may write *Mrs.* in parentheses before the name, the style preferred for professional women, or she may write her married name in parentheses below the signature:

(*style 1*)

(Mrs.) Louise C. Randall

(*style 2*)

*Louise C. Randall
(Mrs. Robert J. Randall)*

A divorced woman may choose to use her unmarried or married surname, alone or with any title:

*Janice Jordan
(Miss) Janice Jordan
(Mrs.) Janice Jordan Taylor*

Of course, any woman may choose to use *Ms.* before her name instead of *Miss* or *Mrs.* In a dictated letter initials are typed at the lower left margin to identify the dictator and the stenographer. If there is an enclosure, it is indicated just under the initials; if more than one by ( ):

FBJ:RHM	FBJ/rhm	FBJ-RHM
Enclosure	Encl.	Enc. (3)

601 FOLDING THE LETTER   The business letter is generally written on one side of a sheet of paper of commercial size, 8½ by 11 inches. When this is to be enclosed in an envelope of the larger size (usually No. 10 —4⅛ by 9½ inches), fold up from the bottom about one third and down from the top slightly less. Place it in the envelope with the free edge at the top and toward the gummed flap (away from you). If the envelope to be used is of the smaller size (usually No. 6¾— 3⅝ by 6½ inches), fold the lower part of the sheet over the upper so that the horizontal crease is slightly below the center; then fold the right-hand part so that the vertical crease is about one third from the right; then fold from the left so that the second vertical crease is slightly less than one third the width of the sheet from the left. Place this in the envelope with the free edge at the top and away from the gummed flap of the envelope (toward you). Be sure that all folds are straight and that all edges are even. The good effect of a letter may be lessened by careless or slovenly folding.

602 OUTSIDE ADDRESS The outside address, or address on the envelope, should be the same in content as the inside address. The first line gives the name and the title of the person addressed, the second line gives the company name; the third line gives the street number, and the fourth line gives the name of the city, the state, and the Zip Code number. The first line should be about the center of the envelope from top to bottom, though some writers prefer that it be slightly below. The name should be correctly spelled (a misspelled name is unforgivable!), and it should be written exactly as the one addressed is known to use it. If a business title is long, it should be placed on a separate line. Abbreviations are optional, but some careful writers avoid them, preferring to write out such words as the names of streets and avenues. An exception is the two-letter state abbreviations authorized by the U.S. Postal Service. These are preferred. An address is usually single-spaced. Special directions, such as General Delivery and Personal, are placed in the lower left corner. The writer's name and address should be in the upper left corner. The following illustration is correct:

```
H. L. Wilson
2145 Valleyroad Avenue South
Springfield, MO  65804




                Mr. Frank W. Whitfield, President
                Ted E. Behr Toy Company, Inc.
                118 Spring Street Northwest
                Atlanta, GA  30304
```

603 APPEARANCE OF THE BUSINESS LETTER A business letter is usually typewritten on a sheet of paper 8½ by 11 inches. Double spacing is used between parts of the letter and between paragraphs. The typing should be so placed on the sheet as to have the margins properly proportioned, with the result that the typed text appears on the sheet much as does a picture properly set in a frame. Even when a letter conforms to all the other requirements of a good letter, its visual appearance also is important. The indented form (opposite) is optional in writing in longhand, but the block form is usual in typing (592). The semiblock style, in which the paragraphs are indented (usually five spaces), is used by many business houses. The following letter is in the semiblock style:

---

126 Park Place
Torrance, CA   90507
May 12, 19--

Mr. J. D. Foster
1770 Pearl Street
Denver, CO   80202

Dear Mr. Foster:

    The information that you gave enabled me to obtain the Greeley contract that I had feared could not be concluded this spring. It was generous of you to take the trouble to assemble this data for me.

    As soon as I have checked the specifications, I will see you for the final details. You will agree with me, I know, that the outlook is promising for us.

    Unless I meet with some unexpected delay, I should have this preliminary work completed by the end of the week. I will let you know the day and the hour to expect me.

Sincerely yours,

L. W. Whitman

L. W. Whitman

LWW:pb

---

126 Park Place
Torrance, CA 90507
May 12, 19--

Mr. J. D. Foster
1770 Pearl Street
Denver, CO 80202

Dear Mr. Foster:

The information that you gave enabled me to

end of the week. I will let you know the day and the hour to expect me.

Sincerely yours,

L. W. Whitman

LWW:pb

L. W. Whitman

604 COMMON TYPES OF BUSINESS LETTERS   There are business letters appropriate to all phases of business; therefore, it would be almost impossible to classify all types. Only the commonly used types can be discussed in a brief book such as this. The following types of business letters are common: **application, order, inquiry and reply, recommendation, introduction, claim, adjustment, acknowledgment and appreciation, advice, collection, congratulation, sales.**

605 LETTER OF APPLICATION   This letter should conform to all requirements of a good business letter (589), and in form (590–603) it should be correct in every detail. No one should do less than one's very best in writing a letter of application. It is in reality a self-sale letter (615) in which the writer is trying to sell services. A short letter of application may consist of three or four paragraphs. The first may mention the source of information about the position, the second may give facts that indicate one's qualifications for holding the position, the third may list references, and the fourth may suggest a possible conference or further communication. But even the conventional form of application may be altered to suit the originality of the writer and the type of position sought. The more individual the message, providing it is always sincere and sensible, the more evident the fitness to fill a position requiring originality.

1735 Magnolia Avenue
Dallas, TX 75201
October 10, 19--

Miss Joan Hamilton
Vogue Food Mart
1917 Houston Street
Dallas, TX 75201

Dear Miss Hamilton:

I have just learned from Mr. Jones, one of
your salespeople, that you wish to employ a reliable
person to help with deliveries and to do odd jobs
about the store after school hours and on Saturdays.
I would like very much to have you consider me for
this work.

I am fourteen years old and am now in the
ninth grade. For three summers I have been with
the Gray Drug Company as delivery boy and general
helper. You may ask Mr. H. W. Gray, the president
of this company, about my qualifications. His
telephone number is 283-8142.

Also, I refer you to Principal H. G. White of
Lowell High School, where I am now a student, and
to Principal W. B. Lake of Roosevelt Junior High
School, the school from which I transferred last
January.

I should be very happy to talk with you. My
telephone number is 314-3657.

Yours very truly,

Harold Roberts

Harold Roberts

606 ORDER The letter ordering goods should be made so clear that it
cannot possibly be misunderstood. It should be exact and complete in
every detail as to quantity, quality, size, catalog number, shape,
style, color, prices, or other items (as a sample of paper or cloth) helping toward exact identification. If the buyer is to pay transportation
charges, he should specify how the order is to be shipped—mail, air-
mail, express, freight, air freight—unless he leaves this matter to the
shipper and so states. The order should give complete instructions for
shipping. Printed order blanks may be used, but in any case no words
should be written in addition to those giving the items and exact instructions relating to the order. Write each item on a separate indented line. If payment is enclosed, state the exact amount and the

form in which it is sent—currency, check, draft, or money order. A credit-card charge must include the name of the card, the account number, and the expiration date of the card. An enclosure may be stapled to the letter, but paper clips should not be used..In the lower left-hand corner should be written *Enclosure, Encl.,* or *Enc.*

---

grant school

1 PARK AVENUE · INDIANAPOLIS, INDIANA 20461·SE 4-5643

January 10, 19___

Grad Supply Co.
4130 Akton Road
Aliquippa, PA 15001

Dear Sir or Madam:

Please send the following "school-auction" items and the sales tags that accompany them. I wish them sent by freight, shipping charges collect.

13 blue-and-white "Grant School" pennants @ $2.25	$19.25
10 leather-grained "Grant School" photo albums @ $4	40.00
144 blue-and-white pencils @ $1.50/doz.	18.00
8 canvas knapsacks with "Grant School" insignia @ $4.75	38.00
120 laminated "Grant School" book covers @ $2.35/doz.	23.50
	$138.75

Our check for $138.75 is enclosed.
Thank you.

Sincerely,

Joy Brookstein

Joy Brookstein,
Student Council Treasurer

---

607 INQUIRY AND REPLY The letter of inquiry should state so precisely what information is wanted that there will be no need for the recipient to have to write for a further explanation of any of its parts. The letter should be as brief as is consistent with courtesy and clarity. When the purpose of the inquiry is of no interest to the recipient, a stamped, self-addressed envelope should be enclosed for reply.

QUATOR PHARMACEUTICALS

2 ROCKEFELLER PLAZA, NEW YORK 10015

July 9, 19--

Mr. Fred Raner
Raner Drugstore
50 Lakewood Drive
Waco, TX   76710

Dear Mr. Raner:

Mr. J. H. Webb has applied for work as
a salesperson in my drugstore. He has referred
me to you as one for whom he has done similar
work. Please give me some general information
as to his fitness for this work. I shall be
grateful to you for this help.

Sincerely yours,

Lisa W. Stevens

LWS-PMB   Lisa W. Stevens

One who receives an inquiry should reply promptly unless it is the type of inquiry not in accord with business ethics. Even when the purpose of the inquiry is of no interest to the recipient, one should give the information as courteously and as fully as if it were of material benefit. One should give not only complete information for every detail of the inquiry but also any additional information that would be of help in the situation. In short, the writer should send the kind of reply he or she would wish for as the inquirer.

Answer to the letter on page 128.

Raner Drugstore

Phone: 817-9711   **R**X   50 Lakewood Drive, Waco, Texas 76710

July 14, 19--

Ms. Lisa W. Stevens
Quator Pharmaceuticals
2 Rockefeller Plaza
New York, NY   10015

Dear Ms. Stevens:

    Mr. J. H. Webb worked for me for two
years, and I found him thoroughly dependable
and efficient at all times. You may be sure
that he will give you excellent service. It
has been very difficult for me to find a salesperson of his ability to replace him since he
moved to your city. I shall appreciate any
consideration you show him.

                              Yours sincerely,

                              Fred Raner

FR/ss   Fred Raner

---

608 RECOMMENDATION   The letter of recommendation may be either personal or general. The personal type, such as the letter of reply above, is addressed to a person or firm by a writer who is recommending someone for a position. It may be written at the request of the one seeking the position or it may be in answer to an inquiry of the prospective employer. It should give concisely and clearly the information that would best help the employer in determining the applicant's fitness for the position.

There should be no vague statements and no overstressing of good qualities so as to make the applicant seem superhuman.

The general "To whom it may concern:" type of recommendation that is placed in the hands of the one recommended is seldom used today, and it does not carry much weight because the tendency of its writer is to give only favorable facts. The employer of today prefers to send a questionnaire to references furnished by the applicant. In this way, information that might be omitted from the general letter of recommendation can be obtained. Of course, failure of a reference to answer the questionnaire or any item of it is interpreted as unfavorable to the candidate. The following, sent in answer to an inquiry not containing a questionnaire, is an example of a longer recommendation than the preceding letter.

DOW INSURANCE

20 EAST 42ᴺᴰ STREET • NEW YORK, N.Y. 10017 • OR 7-0110

June 12, 19--

Mrs. Deborah Jones
Central Insurance Company
1668 Blair Street
Louisville, KY 40201

Dear Mrs. Jones:

It is with pleasure that we recommend Mr. F. H. Warren, about whom you inquired in your letter of June 10. He has been with us for five years, and in that time he has continued to grow in efficiency as an insurance salesperson until he is now among our largest and most consistent producers of quality business. It is because of this development that he now wishes to enter a larger field, such as you can offer him. We realize that his going will mean serious loss for us, but we do not wish to hold him back from the greater opportunities you can provide.

Mr. Warren is a persistent and tireless worker who considers rebuffs only as a challenge to lead him to improve his sales presentation. He is, we sometimes think, unduly impatient at his own reasonable progress; but this may be, after all, a commendable trait.

You will, we feel sure, find many occasions to consider yourselves fortunate if you engage Mr. Warren as a salesperson.

Sincerely yours,

C. C. Dow

CCD:ebe   C. C. Dow, President

609 INTRODUCTION The letter of introduction is used to introduce two of the friends or acquaintances of the writer. It may be given for either business or social reasons, but it should never be given except in all seriousness. One should never give a letter of introduction for business purposes unless one is absolutely sure of the ability and integrity of the person introduced. It would be much better to decline to give the letter than to give less than full approval of the person or to run the risk of introducing one not thoroughly competent and reliable. The message should be simple and as brief as is consistent with completeness and courtesy. The letter, delivered in person by the one introduced, should be enclosed in an unsealed envelope, bearing in proper position the name and full address of the one for whom it is intended and in the lower left-hand corner the words *Introducing Mr._____, Mrs._____, Miss_____, or Ms._____.*

```
                        77 WEST 6 STREET
                        NEW YORK CITY  10024



                        1846 Oak Street
                        Springfield, MO  65801
                        October 6, 19--



    Mr. F. L. Harper
    1720 Market Street
    St. Louis, MO  63155

    Dear Mr. Harper:

        This will introduce you to Ms. Dale Holton, who
    is seeking a position in your city.  I have known
    her for many years, and her training, ability, and
    integrity fit her for excellent service in business
    --the field in which she specialized at the University
    of Missouri, from which she was graduated last June.

        For whatever courtesy or favor you may show this
    young woman, both she and I will be grateful to you.

                        Sincerely yours,

                        James K. Atherton
    JKA:AB
```

610 CLAIM The letter of complaint or claim should always be courteous, dignified, and fair. It should state exactly the cause for complaint and should outline clearly the reasonable adjustment expected. The com-

plainants who impute blame or become sarcastic or abusive only
emphasize their own lack of refinement and make less probable the
adjustment sought. If the impression is given that it is taken for
granted that one is dealing with those who are absolutely honest and
eager to make any reasonable adjustment, the complainant will seldom
fail to get satisfaction. If one has had previous satisfactory dealings
with the company, it is well to mention it to substantiate the expressed
confidence. Most companies are quick to respond favorably to a
justified complaint. The words *claim* or *complaint* are never used in
such a letter.

```
                                    3636 Weldon Street
                                    Dallas, TX   75201
                                    May 6, 19__



          The Glacier Book Company
          340 Vine Street
          Denver, CO 80202

          Gentlemen:

               On May the first I ordered from you one
          copy of Magic Mountain by Dale Warwick.  The
          book arrived by mail today, and I found that
          some of the pages were transposed so that the
          book was not usable.  I wish to return the
          defective copy of the book to you in exchange
          for a perfect copy.

               I shall wait for instructions from you.

               You may be sure that I will appreciate your
          adjusting the matter for me.

                                    Yours very sincerely,

                                    H. C. Bradford

                                    H. C. Bradford
```

611 ADJUSTMENT   The writing of the letter of adjustment sometimes calls
for much diplomacy. Those who write letters of complaint often do so
while they are angry or in a disagreeable mood, but those who answer
them should do so in such a way as to promote good feeling. Even
when the complainant is very unreasonable and abusive, a reply showing courtesy and fairness is usually most effective. When the requested

adjustment is to be made, the letter may be quite simple. An apologetic tone should be avoided, either expressed or implied.

GLACIER
BOOK CO. 340 Vine Street   Denver, Colorado   80202

May 8, 19--

Mr. H. C. Bradford
3636 Weldon Street
Dallas, TX 75201

Dear Mr. Bradford:

    Thank you for calling our attention to the imperfect copy of <u>Magic Mountain</u>. We regret that you have been caused inconvenience, and we assure you that we are glad to adjust the matter. We are sending you by parcel post another copy of the work. We are enclosing with this letter postage for the return of the imperfect volume.

    We appreciate this opportunity of making our service satisfactory and hope to continue to be of service to you in the future.

Very truly yours,

L. W. Glade

LWG:EBK
Encl.

L. W. Glade
President

---

612 ACKNOWLEDGMENT OR ADVICE The receipt of an order or a remittance should be acknowledged at once. If the acknowledgment is of an order, it should refer to the date of the order with other definite reference, such as the order number if there is one, to identify it clearly. It should state when and how the order is to be shipped and should explain in detail if there is to be any delay in filling the order.

If a customer has ordered without having adequate information about the differences in the products available for shipment, the acknowledgment must explain these differences. If the order lacks necessary details, such as size, model, or other specifications, the writer of the acknowledgment should refer to the omission without showing impatience. In short, the acknowledgment should reflect sincere appreciation for the order and so foster a spirit of good will. An acknowledgement of a remittance should be made promptly, and it always should express the sort of sincere appreciation that will encourage further business relations. It often has elements of the sales letter (615). The **letter of advice** is one in which are enclosed the necessary shipping documents that pertain to an order (invoice, packing list, bill of lading, consular documents, bank draft, etc.); it also may be used to give details on the method and time of shipment. The following is an example of the **letter of acknowledgment.**

BELL🔔 20 Office Park Drive, Birmingham, Ala. 35223
Sporting Goods

March 3, 19--

Mr. Robert Leewright
325 Central Drive
Lancaster, PA 17601

Dear Mr. Leewright:

Thank you for your order of February 27 for our X214--7½-ft. spinning rod and L-340 spinning reel with 200 yards of 6-pound-test monofilament line. These will be shipped to you by express prepaid today.

You asked about our automatic reel A160 for fly rods. This will easily hold 25 yards of GAF line, but not 35 yards as you specify. May I suggest our A260 Automatic Reel, described in the enclosed circular? This is one of the finest reels on the market and has proved very popular. I believe it would fill the needs you indicate in your letter. The circular contains a convenient order form for your use.

Your order is very much appreciated, and we hope that we may continue to be of service to you.

Very truly yours,

Norma Roberts

NR:RM   Norma Roberts
Encl.   Sales Manager

VILIONS

DEPARTMENT STORE

4 EAST RIDGE AVENUE · WOOD, NEW JERSEY 07450

652-5252

October 18, 19_____

Mr. J. F. Grant
615 West Fifth Avenue
Wood, NJ 07450

Dear Mr. Grant:

What do you think we should do?

We have a small account that remains unpaid. We
have sent two reminders. We are sincerely interested in keeping the good will of all our customers;
yet we cannot continue to build up a large collection
expense. What would you suggest that we do?

This small account is yours. It is only $46.28, but
it is six weeks overdue. You know the value of our
credit privilege, and I am sure you want to retain
it. Our spring sales will soon place a wide selection of fine bargains on our shelves, and you will
find your credit with us a valuable convenience.

Our extension of time on your account has already
been most liberal. In justice to our other customers
and as a matter of fair play, won't you settle this
account at once and retain your good credit standing?

I am enclosing an addressed, postage-free envelope
for your convenience. Please make use of it now to
send us your check. It will be appreciated.

Sincerely yours,

Olin Hiebert

OH:mr   Olin Hiebert
Enc.   Credit Manager

613 COLLECTION The writer of the successful collection letter must use
tact. The task of collecting the money and of retaining the good will
and continued patronage of the customer is difficult. With all the
courtesy and consideration, however, the collector must not leave the
impression of being easygoing. Collectors should not be too friendly or
too sympathetic and, above all, should not be apologetic. Firmness
should always be apparent.

614 CONGRATULATION   The message of congratulations in business need not be restricted to commercial relationships only. Since it is prompted more by courtesy than by obligation, it calls for no reply. It is, of course, very similar to the congratulatory letter of friendship (622), but it should follow the business-letter form. Thus its tone is often rather formal, depending on the personal relationships involved. The following message is an example of this type of letter.

Newport Industries⎯⎯⎯⎯ 11 Broadway, New York, New York 10006

October 18, 19--

Mrs. Josephine Smith
4903 Ellis Avenue
Chicago, IL 60607

Dear Mrs. Smith:

As soon as I heard of your election to the
board of directors of your firm, I felt I must
write you to let you know how happy I am in
your advancement.

All of your friends have felt that, in spite
of the great difficulties you have faced in
your climb up through the ranks, the outstand-
ing ability we all recognized in you could not
go unacknowledged. This advancement is certainly
your due, and I think your firm should also be
congratulated on taking advantage more fully of
your exceptional talents.

                              Sincerely yours,

                              Charles E. Hodgson

                              Charles E. Hodgson
CEH:mr   President

Target The Magazine for Teens
1 Charles Lane Nashville, TN 37203

April 14, 19____

Mr. Gerald Bovell
1550 Fairmount Ave.
Palo Alto, CA 94304

Dear Mr. Bovell:

Do you like to do more than just follow the latest fad?

Then you should know about Target, the magazine aimed at
smart teens who like to know what is going on in the world
of entertainment and why.

Each month will bring you in-depth interviews with stars
that make the music world happen. In addition, there'll
be many fascinating articles and reviews on the latest
books, movies, and sports events.

A special feature, a consumer guide, will explore the
latest fads and trends that affect you—and your wallet.
Before you buy that pair of designer jeans, you'll want
to check our rating system for quality and price
comparisons.

We won't let you down. Our editorial board is made
up of teens themselves—who know what's up, what's in,
and what's around.

Why not join us as a charter subscriber? If you send in
the coupon, you can get a year's worth of Target for half
the newsstand price. Send in your order today. You'll
be right on target!

                          Sincerely,

                          Terry Fenmore

                          Terry Fenmore,
                          Editor

615 SALES   The sales letter is generally considered not only the most important of all business letters but also the most difficult to write. The requirements of the business letter vary with individual types, but every good sales letter must accomplish these four things: **attract attention, arouse desire, secure conviction,** and **induce action—brevity,** the "you" **attitude,** and **completeness** are correlative with these four. To do these things best, the letter should conform to all requirements of the business letter (589). A good opening sentence attracts the attention and causes the reader to continue reading.

Social Correspondence

616 SOCIAL LETTERS   The social letter varies from the informal letter of friendship to the most formal note. Social letters may be divided into these groups: letters of **friendship, courtesy, formality.**

617 LETTERS OF FRIENDSHIP   The letter of friendship may be light in tone or dignified, and its style should be conversational. Even its form is less conventional than that of the business letter, and the stationery may vary to suit the taste of the writer. However, the general make-up is similar to that of the business letter, except that the **inside address** (594) is usually omitted. The **heading** (591), **salutation** (595), **complimentary close** (599), **signature** (600), and **outside address** (602) are similar to those of the business letter. If an inside address is included, it is placed in the upper right-hand corner or, especially on short notes, at the left-hand margin below the signature.

Because the letter of friendship is usually written in longhand, some writers prefer to use the indented form (592) in the letter parts. The punctuation (593) of the parts is the same as for the business letter, except that a comma (instead of the colon) follows the salutation. The salutation, complimentary close, and signature are not so formal; these should be in keeping with the relationship of the correspondents. Such salutations as the following are appropriate: *Dear Fred, Dear Mr. Hilton, Dear Aunt Mary.*

INFORMAL NOTE OF FRIENDSHIP:

> 6188 Maple St.
> Dallas, TX 75201
> May 15, 19—

Dear Ruth,

    It would be just great to hear from you! Of course you must be very busy getting ready for college, but do let me know if you can spend the last week in August with me before you leave. If you can come for my birthday, August 31, you will be the best part of the celebration. I am having a number of friends over that I would like you to meet.

    I heard that you are going to be in a special pre-law program. You always did have such a logical, well-organized mind!

    With my interest in science, I've been thinking about a career in medicine. Of course, I have a while to think about it, since I have another year of high school.

    Do you remember the playhouse in our yard? I've converted it into a workroom where I've been doing pottery such as bowls and vases. You must take one with you when you go to college. Please write and let me know your plans. I hope to see you soon.

Sincerely,

Betts

REPLY TO PRECEDING INFORMAL INVITATION:

1122 Maple Wood
Houston, TX 77002
May 27, 19—

Dear Betts,

It was a nice surprise to get your letter. I was so busy with school and my part-time job at a department store that my correspondence got pushed aside. Thank you for your invitation to spend the last week in August with you. I would love to come. I can hardly wait to see you again! It would be lovely to meet your friends—I enjoy social occasions, especially birthday parties. We have a lot to talk about, from career plans to hobbies, and I am just counting the weeks until our visit.

Fondly,

Ruth

There are some points of the informal letter on which writers are not agreed. For instance, some omit the address in the heading altogether while others place it at the left below the signature; some even omit the heading, although this is a practical reminder of the address.

618 **LETTER OF COURTESY** The letter of courtesy, as defined in Clark's *When You Write a Letter*, is "the letter written not in reply to another letter nor yet to elicit a reply of any sort, but simply as an act of politeness and thoughtfulness to acknowledge a kindness or an obligation or to let one's friends or acquaintances know that one was aware of their sorrows and their successes, of their comings and goings, and that one had a real personal interest in these." Of the many classes of letters of this kind, only these four need be discussed: **acknowledgment, appreciation, condolence,** and **congratulation.**

619 **ACKNOWLEDGMENT OR THANKS** There are many types of acknowledgment (612) that duty and courtesy demand of us. It is obligatory that we acknowledge receipt of a letter, a present, an unusual courtesy, a favor, an offer, a request, or an invitation. There are many persons, however, including many young people, who do not respond to this social obligation. They should know, though, that this failure of acknowledgment brands them as thoughtless or ungrateful.

Buffalo, TX 75831
July 15, 19—

Dear Mr. and Mrs. Moore,

    Thank you for your hospitality last week. I felt right at home at your summer cottage. The meals were great, the bed was comfortable, and most of all, the company was terrific. I'll never forget the surprise birthday barbecue party you had for me by the lake— and the surprise thunderstorm that went with it!

    My parents and I hope that you will pay a visit to Buffalo soon. We'd love to show you around our neck of the woods.

Sincerely,
Henry Jones

620 APPRECIATION There is perhaps no other form of letter that has greater possibilities of bringing joy to both writer and recipient than the letter of appreciation. Yet it is a type that is neglected because we human beings seem more inclined to condemn than to praise. Dr. Clark (see 618) says, "When there is something which can be criticized adversely or found fault with, we jump at it [letter writing] with alacrity, but when we meet something worthy of praise, we say nothing." The expression of appreciation should be simple and sincere, with no implication of flattery.

80 Federal Street
Boston, MA 02109
October 24, 19—

Dear Grandma,

    Well, I'm finally getting used to my first "grown-up" job and my first apartment. These past few months have been pretty hectic and exciting, but I want you to know that I haven't forgotten how much you've helped me get where I am. It sounds a little corny, but I don't think I could have got through college without your encouragement. When I felt like giving up, your advice about doing what's best for me helped me see things in a new light.

    I'm sure you know how I feel about you. But I just wanted to put some of these thoughts into writing. Thanks again for everything. I'll see you at Thanksgiving!

Love,
Louise

621 CONDOLENCE A letter of condolence (sympathy) should always be written in longhand. It should be short and reflect the sincerity of the writer. Avoid reference to death or sorrow. Often there is no occasion for a letter of condolence from young people, as letters sent by one's parents are usually adequate. But there are times when a young person may feel the need to send some expression of his own feelings in a simple note such as the following:

> Dear Fred:
> My deepest sympathy goes to you in the loss of your mother. I shall always remember how friendly and encouraging she was to me when I came over to your house.
>
> Most sincerely,
>
> *Tom*

There are occasions when one person may be selected to write a letter of condolence for a group or class:

> Dear Mr. and Mrs. Smith:
> The Ninth Grade has asked me to express to you our deepest sympathy and the feeling of loss we all have. Fred was a valued companion to all of us and we feel privileged to have known him.
>
> Most sincerely,
>
> *Mildred Mason*
> Class president

622 CONGRATULATION Sincere, appropriate words at times of successful achievement make for greater happiness in both the business (614) and social world:

> 356 Cochran Road
Lexington, KY 40501
February 3, 19—
>
> Dear Karen,
> I had no idea that you'd won the Teen Monthly Young Writers' Contest until I opened the February issue on my way home from the dentist. I wanted to jump up and tell everybody on the bus that my oldest friend is a famous writer! (I did manage to control myself until I got home.)

Karen, why didn't you tell me—your first fan and critic—
that you entered the contest? Your last letter said nothing about
writing that short story. Anyway, I'm already beginning to write
down my memories of our childhood together. I want to be ready
for your first biography.

Mom and Dad are happy for you and say they're not surprised at all. *I* was, though. And I hope there will be more surprises
like that in the future.

Love,

Mandy

623 **FORMAL INVITATION, ACCEPTANCE, REGRET**   The formal invitation is
always written in the third person. It has neither heading, inside address, salutation, complimentary close, nor signature. Only a few abbreviations such as *Ms.*, *Mr.*, *Mrs.*, and *Dr.* are permitted. Numbers
other than house numbers are written out. The response to the invitation must be written in the same rigid form and must contain the
information given by it.

INVITATION:

Mr. and Mrs. Henry L. Black
request the pleasure of
Miss Mildred Ware's
company at dinner
on Wednesday evening, the fourth of June
at seven o'clock
421 Glendale Road

ACCEPTANCE:

Miss Mildred Ware
accepts with pleasure
Mr. and Mrs. Henry L. Black's
kind invitation for dinner
on Wednesday evening, the fourth of June
at seven o'clock

REGRET:

Miss Mildred Ware
regrets that she is unable to accept
Mr. and Mrs. Henry L. Black's
kind invitation for dinner
on Wednesday evening, the fourth of June

624 **TELEGRAM**   A telegram should be as brief as is consistent with
clearness, which is absolutely essential. Telegrams are costly, and
every word over the minimum increases the cost; but the elimination
of words at the expense of clearness is poor economy. In all domestic

telegrams the date, address, and signature are sent without charge. Each word, long or short, is counted. Thus it is economical to use one long word when it conveys the idea of two or more short ones. Punctuation marks are sent free. The word *stop* may be used between sentences for clarity, but it is counted as one word each time it is used. A standard abbreviation like C.O.D. is counted as one word. When figures or mixed groups of figures, letters, and signs (as 65%) are used, each group of five is counted as one word. Mailgrams, cablegrams, and radiograms are counted by a somewhat different method.

```
MUST SELL PROPERTY BY NOON TOMORROW.
WIRE OFFER BY THEN.

BEST CASH OFFER $100,000 STOP
$10,000 BINDER IN MAIL
```

Newspaper Writing

625 Newspaper writing includes **news stories, headlines, feature stories, interviews, editorials, announcements, syndicated columns,** and miscellaneous articles.

626 NEWS STORY   The news story tells recent important or interesting events. It usually begins with a summarizing paragraph called the lead, which should answer most of these questions: *Who? When? Where? What? Why? How?* This paragraph should be accurate and concise, and it should contain the main facts so that the reader need not proceed further unless details are wanted, which are given in the order of their importance in the paragraphs following the lead. Some newspapers are beginning to break away from this conventional lead-paragraph technique.

627 SUGGESTIONS FOR WRITING NEWS

1. Accuracy is of first importance. Get all the facts right. Be especially careful to spell personal and place names accurately.
2. Tell the story simply. Use specific rather than general terms. Do not use unnecessary words.
3. Tell facts only, never let it reflect the opinions of the reporter or editor.
4. In quoting, use the exact words of the person quoted. Never quote anything that would imply ignorance on the part of the speaker unless there is a clearly justifiable reason for doing so. In short, one should use tact and common sense in writing news just as in other forms of writing.
5. In preparing copy, follow exactly the instructions provided by the editor. A newspaper or journal usually has a style sheet that tells

which of certain alternative correct spellings and forms of capitalization and punctuation have been adopted by the paper for its
own use.

628 HEADLINES   Headlines tell the news in a few words and guide the
readers in finding the news they wish to read. The main facts of the
story should be emphasized in the headlines. Short words are pref-
erable. Do not use *a, an,* and *the.* Headline writers must count the
letters in each line written and rewrite it until the length meets
specifications in the style sheet of the newspaper. The large headlines contain several sections, each of which is called a **deck.** The top
deck tells the most important fact. Each deck should have a verb, and
no deck should end with a preposition. The present tense (191) and
the active voice (184) are preferred.

629 FEATURE STORY   The feature story includes a variety of types of writing other than that used in news stories. It may be a brief human-
interest story suggested by some event introduced as news or a fashion
forecast or a book or play review; or it may be a long, informative
article such as those that appear in Sunday magazine sections. Re-
porters may use a more individual style in writing feature stories than
in reporting news and may sometimes state their own impressions
and feelings or use quotations. Feature stories are frequently distinguished by headlines different from those used for news stories; they
may also be printed in boxes.

630 REPORT OF INTERVIEW   One who intends to report an interview (see
648) should have clearly in mind the questions to be asked. These
questions should be asked tactfully, and the answers should be recorded accurately for later writing. As few notes as possible should be
taken in the presence of the one interviewed, and, for this reason, the
report ought to be written immediately after the interview. In the lead
of such a story, a quotation from the one interviewed may be used; if
so it must be verbatim and have, if at all possible, the approval of the
interviewee to avoid error. Also, the interviewee's name should be
featured, as well as some of his or her characteristics. The subject of
the interview or its purpose should likewise be featured.

631 EDITORIALS   An editorial is an essay (640) on some subject of interest
to the public. All writers are free to use their own individual styles. The
editorial usually has a title instead of headlines and a lead. Its purpose
is generally to present an argument, to entertain, or occasionally to
give information. The argumentative type is usually on a subject of
public interest and is often a plea for some reform. The facts upon
which such an argument is based should be carefully verified by reliable
authorities. The editorial that means to entertain is often a kind of
informal essay and is usually less serious in style than the other forms,

being sometimes satirical or humorous. Polemical writing is a style completely at variance with the intent and scope of good editorial writing.

SAVE OUR LIBRARIES

We read with interest a recent article in this paper about the amount of television watching among teenagers. It is ironic that as parents and educators complain about too much TV, the city decides that the public library is one of those "nonessential" city services and threatens to reduce its budget drastically. We strenuously oppose these plans. A healthy library is necessary for the future of this community. For the young and old alike, it offers a quiet haven where one can be alone—to browse, to read, or just to think. More than that, it is a guarantee that no one, no matter how poor, will be cut off from the world of books. And in these times, when a new book of fiction can cost fifteen or twenty dollars, we need that guarantee desperately.

This city cannot afford to have its local branches open just three or four days a week, with shortened hours and a dwindling collection of books. It is a disgrace when working students aren't free during the few hours the library is open or when they can't write a research paper because the library does not have the books. Just as a public education is every citizen's right, so is a well-stocked, free, and *open* public library.

632 **ANNOUNCEMENTS** A form of writing for publication that is important but not extensive is the announcement, which should be brief, clear, emphatic, and free from exaggeration. Kipling's six honest serving men (p. 115) will prove helpful in the writing of announcements.

The Research Paper

633 **SOURCE MATERIAL** Choose a subject in which you are interested and which is not too broad in scope. Once you have chosen your subject, consult the Card Catalog and *Reader's Guide to Periodical Literature* in your library to find out what reference material is available. Note the copyright date; some of the material may be out of date for your purpose.

Keep in mind the difference between original and secondary sources of material. For example, in writing about a person, letters would be an original source of information, and a printed collection of letters will generally be as good as an original source (keeping in mind the fact that letters may have sometimes been edited in a reprint edition). A secondary source would be the opinions of another author about the person under discussion. For important papers, original sources should be used when available.

634 THE SOURCE-CARD TECHNIQUE List each source on a separate card—usually 3 x 5 inches. Include—

1. **Author's name.** Give last name first, then given names, or the editor's name followed by the abbreviation *ed.* When no author is given, list the title first. Names of authors other than the first author listed may be given in normal order.

2. **Title.** Underline the title of a book, magazine, or newspaper and put quotation marks around the title of an article or chapter.

3. **Publication data.** For book titles include the city where published, name of publisher, and copyright date. For magazines or journals use the date of issue and page numbers.

4. **Library call number.** For books include the call number so that you don't have to look this up again. Here are samples of source cards for a book, an article in a magazine, and an article in an encyclopedia:

```
913   Alcock, Leslie
 A    Was This Camelot?
      Excavation at Cadbury
      Castle, 1966-1970
      New York: Stein and Day, 1972
```

```
      Wickerd, Ron, and Fran Wickerd
      "In Quest of King Arthur"
      Travel, Vol. 136 (September
      1971), pp. 54-61
```

```
      "Arthurian Legend"
      The New Encyclopaedia
      Britannica, 1985 edition
      Micropaedia, Vol. I, pp. 603-4
```

635 OUTLINES Start with a working outline showing clearly the topics you expect to write about. As you gather material, you may want to change this outline, omitting some topics about which you find little source material and adding others that appear to be interesting or more significant. After you have gathered all your information, you may make your final outline (579–580) to guide your writing.

636 TAKING NOTES The best way to gather material is to take notes on 3 x 5-inch or larger cards for which you have a file box. These cards will enable you to organize your material and refer readily to your information on each topic as you write. The following are helpful rules for taking notes:

1. **Use a separate card for each note.** This permits you to file your cards under the proper topic. Sometimes more than one card will be necessary for a topic.

2. **Take thorough notes on all of the points you plan to cover.** Many students find that three or four good notes are required for every page of the research paper. Don't keep repeating information even if it is found in different books, and do not take notes on material you do not plan to use.

3. **List the topic the note refers to.** The topic is best placed at the top left corner of the card. This enables you to refer to your notes quickly as you write and helps you to organize your material.

4. **Be accurate.** Your notes must report facts, figures, opinions, and quotations accurately. Double-check every word and every figure with your source.

5. **Mark each direct quotation clearly.** Put quotation marks around each quotation. In your manuscript short quotations will be shown with quotation marks; longer quotations will be shown by leaving larger margins (510). Take down the exact words, punctuation, and capitalization. Use three dots to indicate the omission of parts of a quotation (488). Use direct quotations only if you plan to give the exact opinion of an authority or if the same idea cannot possibly be expressed in your own words. Too many quotations will make a very weak paper. Express your own ideas in your own way.

6. **Identify the source and give the page reference for each note.** This information will be necessary for your footnotes (638) and your bibliography (639). You should have some key for connecting your note card with its source card. You may make up your own abbreviation for each source card, or you may number your source cards in order and then put the proper source number on each note card.

637 WRITING THE PAPER When you have your purpose and viewpoint clearly in mind, you may start by writing an introduction. Otherwise, save your introduction to the last and start with your first topic. Follow your final outline in arranging your notes. In this way your material will be logically organized, but you still must supply transitions (549)—sometimes using whole paragraphs—to make your paper a unified, coherent whole. Try to make your sentences sound smooth and connected, not a miscellaneous assortment hastily thrown together. A first draft may be written rapidly, but be very careful of the mechanics of your writing in your revised final copy.

638 FOOTNOTES   General information—such as you have found in a number of different books—usually doesn't have to be credited. But specific information—statistics, direct quotations, opinions of experts— should be credited. You give credit in two ways. If the source is clear, you may mention it briefly in a sentence within your paragraph: "As H. C. Lodge says in *Science* for May 22, 1977, . . ." But usually a footnote is best for complete reference to your source. At the end of material to be credited, put a number slightly above the line to correspond to the number you will use for your footnote at the bottom of the page. Numbers usually run consecutively throughout an entire paper, but it is not incorrect to start over with each new page.

Material to be credited should be taken accurately from your note cards, and you can take from your source cards all the data necessary for your footnote credit. The following are examples of forms you may use for articles and books. Since you will have a full bibliography, you may omit publication data from your footnotes if your teacher approves.

BOOK

> [1]
> Elizabeth Jenkins, The Mystery of King Arthur (New York: Coward, McCann, and Geoghegan, Inc., 1975), p. 28.

MAGAZINE ARTICLE

> [2]
> Leslie Alcock, "By South Cadbury is That Camelot . . . ," Antiquity, Vol. XLI (March 1967), p. 52.

ENCYCLOPEDIA ARTICLE

> [3]
> "Arthurian Romances," The Encyclopedia Americana, International Edition, 1985, Vol. 2, p. 409.

When you refer several times to the same source, it is not necessary to repeat the entire footnote. Suppose you need to credit an article the second time before you refer to any other source. Simply write *Ibid.* (meaning "in the same place") as your footnote, adding a page number if the page is different:

> [4] Ibid., p. 71.

Some writers use *Loc. cit.* (in the place cited) when the page number is the same. If another footnote has intervened, write the author's name and *op. cit.* ("in the work cited"), or just use the author's name:

```
5                              5
  Jenkins, op. cit., p. 71.     Jenkins, p.71.
```

If the author is not given, a shortened reference to the previous source may be used:

```
6
Encyclopedia Americana, p. 410.
```

639 BIBLIOGRAPHY At the end of your research paper give a bibliography of all the printed material you have used in preparing your paper. Usually your bibliography will include the same works that you credited in your footnotes, but you may list additional helpful works that you consulted but did not have to credit. The form of your bibliographical entries is the same as that in your source cards. These should be alphabetized and copied accurately.

```
Alcock, Leslie, "By South Cadbury is That
    Camelot . . ." Antiquity, Vol. XLI, March 1967,
    pp. 50-53.

"Arthurian Romances." The Encyclopedia Americana:
    International Edition, 1985, Vol. 2, pp. 409-
    410.

Ashe, Geoffrey, in association with Debrett's
    Peerage, The Discovery of King Arthur. Garden
    City, N.Y.: Anchor Press/Doubleday, 1985.

Jenkins, Elizabeth. The Mystery of King Arthur.
    New York: Coward, McCann, and Geoghegan, Inc.,
    1975.
```

Writing Essays

640 ESSAYS The term *essay* is a rather broad one, for it includes all forms of short creative writing inspired by personal reactions. Inexperienced writers, however, should restrict their attempts at essay writing to one type—the informal, or familiar, essay. This form is the expression of the writer's own thoughts on his chosen subject. The subject and the style of the informal essay may vary to suit the writer. The style of the writing, though, is in keeping with the mood of the theme. Some suggestions offered for writing the informal essay are: *make your reader share your ideas and understand their relation, choose appropriate words, use a simple style, use quotations and figures of speech, vary your sentences, revise for clearness and effectiveness.*

Oral Communication

641 **Oral communication** is made up largely of conversation, the most informal of the types of communication; but it includes speaking in public, which may vary greatly in its degree of formality.

Conversation

642 Conversational language is normally less formal than that which is written, even in letters; but the conversationalist meets with dangers not encountered by the writer. Here are some suggestions for those who would like to be good conversationalists:

1. **Be a good listener.** Perhaps there is no more effective way of gaining the reputation of being a good conversationalist than by listening attentively. Be interested and never interrupt.

2. **Get the other's viewpoint.** Do your best to see things as the other person sees them. This is not easy, but it is important.

3. **Learn the other person's interests.** Show interest in the other's interests, not just in expressing your own.

4. **Respect the opinions of others.** Though you may not agree with another person's opinions, respect that person's right to have them.

5. **Never argue.** There is nothing to gain by arguing in ordinary conversation, but there is much to lose.

6. **Make no reference to the other person's weakness.**

7. **Acknowledge excellence in others.** All people have superior points that deserve recognition.

8. **Stimulate the other's feeling of importance.** Honestly and sincerely encourage the other's self-respect.

9. **Say the other person's name.** But be sure to use the name naturally and not as if for effect, and be doubly sure to pronounce it correctly. No one ever quite forgives the person who mispronounces or misspells one's name.

10. **Do not be a know-it-all.** Perhaps the most unpopular of all conversationalists is the know-it-all—the person who tops every tale, no matter how tall—the person who boasts about having been everywhere and seen everything.

11. **Do not be gloomy.** Do not dwell on mournful or depressing incidents or predictions. Try at least to appear cheerful and hopeful.

12. **Do not be cynical.** Refrain from expressing the views of a disparager—a doubter—an unbeliever in sincerity or nobility.

13. **Never be catty.** Those who make catty (slyly spiteful—as the dictionary says) remarks cannot hope to have friends.

14. **Do not be overcorrect.** Use good but natural speech, and do not overdo correctness by becoming finicky about unimportant usages. In your community use the language of your community.

15. **Be genuinely courteous.** Be tactful and courteous always. In a group, make everyone feel at ease. Include everyone in your conversation, and do not talk over the heads of anyone present. Encourage those who are reticent or shy. They may often be the most interesting talkers.

16. **Be able to make correct introductions.** One should be able to introduce oneself and to introduce others properly and tactfully. Any good book on etiquette will serve to refresh one's memory on special points of introduction, but ordinarily one can easily remember that the boy is presented to the girl, the man to the woman, and the younger person to the older person. John Jones may introduce himself to another by saying, "I am John Jones." He may introduce two others, a boy and a girl, by saying, "Mildred Gray, this is Bob Jones." If Bob is seated, he rises at the introduction and says, "I'm happy to meet you." Mildred need not rise if seated. Men, on being introduced, always shake hands. Today women often choose to do so, too. The forms of introductions are more or less fixed, but informality need not be ruled out.

Speaking Before an Audience

643 Few of us become professional public speakers, but there are occasions in the life of everyone when the ability to address an audience effectively is highly advantageous. General suggestions include those on the **appearance** of the speaker, the **voice**, the **language**, the preparation of the **speech**, and the **delivery**:

1. **Appearance of the Speaker.** The speaker should be neatly and appropriately dressed. In facing an audience, one should assume an easy, natural position and try to be as calm and comfortable as possible. After a slight pause, one should begin to speak. One should look at one's audience without special attention to individuals. Try to concentrate solely on the message—in this way one can avoid being self-conscious about where to place one's hands or feet. If notes are used, they should be typed on small cards, so that they will not attract the attention of the audience.

2. **Voice.** The speaker should use natural tones and should speak loudly enough to be heard distinctly by all. If there is a microphone, speak directly toward it. The voice should be well modulated with no tendency toward monotonous singsong. Every word should be pronounced correctly (675) and clearly.

3. **Language.** Use correct language in speaking before an audience, especially in giving a formal address. Errors in speech that pass unnoticed in a talk with friends will sound awkward when spoken before an audience. One's language should be appropriate to the topic and the occasion. On a serious or formal occasion, avoid slang and colloquial speech used when speaking with friends. In an informal talk, one can speak in a more natural, relaxed manner. A good speaker is always tactful—he or she shows some consideration for the audience. A speech that shows com-

mon sense and has varied sentences and a good message can win the attention of any audience.

4. **Preparation of the Speech.** In preparing a speech, one usually has in mind to instruct, to convince, or to entertain. Accordingly every part of the speech should be appropriate to its purpose. It should also be appropriate to the occasion on which it is given and to the audience. The speaker shouldn't memorize the address, although it should have been carefully outlined in notes. The outline should consist of an introduction, main message, and conclusion.

5. **Delivery of the Speech.** Be sure the beginning is forceful. The first sentence often determines the whole effect of an address. Never begin a speech with an apology, no matter how poorly prepared you are. If jokes or humorous stories are used, be sure they have a purpose and that they are appropriate. If you cannot tell a joke well, omit it. One bad joke will spoil the effect of a good speech. Be sincere, and above all, be enthusiastic— enthusiasm is contagious. There is no excuse to speak listlessly and disinterestedly, even in a good cause, for it always hurts the cause it should promote. Be sure to stop promptly when your message is ended. In making an announcement, be brief; but make sure your announcement is clear and understandable.

Other Forms of Oral Communication

644 THE TELEPHONE   Only general suggestions for the use of the telephone may be offered here:

1. Be sure to exercise the same courtesy and consideration in using the telephone that you would if you were talking directly with the person. This means, of course, that the voice should be properly modulated and that there must be no indication of indifference, inattention, hurry, impatience, or annoyance.

2. Be alert, responsive, and courteous under even the most trying circumstances.

3. The person who initiates the call should terminate it. Therefore, it is impolite for the receiver to conclude the conversation unless there is good reason for doing so.

4. Do not prolong a telephone conversation on trivial matters when someone is waiting to use the telephone.

5. Do not use a business telephone for prolonged personal visiting.

6. Do not use another's private telephone without asking permission.

7. Do not, by distracting noise or actions, disturb someone who is using a telephone.

8. Never eavesdrop on the telephone conversations of others.

645 ORAL BOOK REPORT Oral reports can give you valuable experience in expressing your thoughts clearly and coherently. This skill has widespread applications, from business presentations down to casual conversations about movies. There are few hard and fast rules for making a book report. Begin by naming the book, its author, the publisher and date of publication. Then:

1. Explain the purpose of the book.
2. Describe the characters and the setting (when reviewing fiction).
3. Compare the work with others of a similar nature.
4. Read brief extracts from the book to indicate its style; but they should be carefully selected and read well. (Do not read without prior practice with the text.)
5. Explain why you like or dislike the book.
6. Use good English without "being bookish." Make your report clear and enjoyable.

646 STORYTELLING Storytelling at its best is a fine art. Few of us become artists in this field, but everyone should learn to tell stories at least reasonably well. In addition to the suggestions offered under 643, there are others which good storytellers follow.

1. Plunge immediately into the story.
2. Give the events in their logical order.
3. Vary your sentence structure, and put life into your expression.
4. Suit your mood to that of the story, but remember that tactful humor is seldom inappropriate.
5. Make your conclusion strong and imaginative.

647 ANECDOTES Everyone should learn to tell anecdotes well. A bit of artful humor lends tang to any conversation, and the effectiveness of a public speaker often depends on one's skill at using appropriate anecdotes. Here are a few general suggestions:

1. The anecdote should be suited to the listeners and to the occasion.
2. It should be brief.
3. It should have a point, revealed only with the conclusion—the punch line as it is called. Rehearse the exact wording of your final sentence.
4. Use common sense in your selection of anecdotes.
5. Tell your anecdote *effectively* once, but don't repeat any part of it.
6. Don't suggest that your audience has heard the story before.

648 INTERVIEW An interviewer should introduce himself or herself and
then make clear the purpose of the meeting. If the interviewee is
seeking a position, all qualifications should be stated frankly, accurately, and confidently without seeming boastful. After the meeting
the interviewee should thank the interviewer, whether the outcome
of the interview is favorable or not.

649 DISCUSSION Friendly, intelligent discussion is one of the most en-
lightening forms of communication. Your teacher will help you plan
interesting discussions in class. There is no lack of excellent subjects
for such discussion: community affairs, current events, a story, a play,
a poem, or some popular book.

In a good discussion everyone is interested and everyone wants to
talk. Everyone has studied the topic and has something to say. There
will be strong opinions and perhaps some excitement. This is as it
should be; a discussion should be fun and should lead to self-expression. This does not mean that loss of temper or rude interruption is
an acceptable form of self-expression. Excitement does not excuse dis-
courtesy. Loud argument and squabbles destroy discussion. The following are suggested rules for good discussion.

1. Choose a topic of real interest to the group.

2. Give everyone a chance to talk.

3. Listen to what others say so that you can contribute to the line of
discussion. Avoid repeating what someone else has said.

4. Stick to the subject.

5. Don't interrupt.

6. Show respect for others' opinions, but don't be shy in expressing
your own opinion.

7. Be courteous in correcting a statement you think is erroneous.

8. Don't argue about facts; look them up.

To make sure that everyone who wishes to talk has a fair chance,
the group should have a chairperson. The discussion may be largely
informal, but all students should "address the chair" and wait until
the chairperson speaks their names. This procedure avoids the un-
profitable situation in which everyone tries to talk at once. A good
chairperson will also keep the speakers on the subject.

650 GIVING INFORMATION People should train themselves to ask for and
to give information briefly, accurately, and courteously. In giving information, as for instance, on how to find a place, it is often necessary
to repeat for emphasis; but too much repetition confuses.

651 ANNOUNCEMENTS AND BRIEF TALKS Everyone should be able to make clear, effective announcements and to make creditable short talks before audiences. Every student should be able to announce effectively a coming event, make a rousing pep talk, introduce a speaker, or make a nomination or a presentation speech. In all these, one should remember to stick to the main purpose, be brief, give facts, and make a strong beginning and closing.

652 CLUBS AND OTHER ORGANIZATIONS The rules that govern club meetings are so familiar to students that detailed instructions are not needed here. You have, no doubt, taken part in many school organizations. Under the guidance of your teacher, you have become familiar with the working rules of groups. If there are points on which you are not clear, any standard work, such as *Robert's Rules of Order, Newly Revised; The Sturgis Standard Code of Parliamentary Procedure,* or L. W. Bridge's *Book of Parliamentary Procedure,* will set you right. A summary of the essential rules for regular club work would include these: *How to call a meeting to organize a group, how to nominate and select officers, how to make a motion, how to second a motion, how to call a meeting to order, how committees are appointed, how the chairperson of a committee is selected.* A knowledge of these rules coupled with good judgment and consideration for others will enable you to do effective, enjoyable club work.

7

Choice of Words

"But 'glory' doesn't mean 'a nice knock-down argument,' " Alice objected.

"When I use a word," Humpty Dumpty said, in rather a scornful tone, "it means just what I choose it to mean—neither more nor less."

From *Through the Looking-Glass*
by Lewis Carroll

Standards of Diction

653 LANGUAGE IS GROWING A living language is constantly changing. Its standards of correctness are established by those who are considered its most authoritative users. Inexperienced writers and speakers especially should stay within the limits of those standards and use only words that are sanctioned by best authority. However, this standard of correctness may vary with the form of expression in which it is found. The formal literary type of expression would be out of place in a more informal situation requiring a colloquial (657) type of expression. The report of a football game kept to the standard required for a formal essay would no doubt be rather dull reading. Even the standard required for the less formal kinds of writing might be altogether out of place in conversation.

Good English, then, is that in which the type of expression and the occasion or purpose of a communication are appropriate to one another. *Diction* as used here refers to the choice of words for their accuracy, clarity, variety, and effectiveness. It does not refer to its secondary meaning, the manner of speaking—that is, the pronunciation and enunciation of words—by public speakers and singers.

Varieties of Diction

654 Some types of expression are avoided by the best writers and speakers. Other types are acceptable when appropriate to the situation. An understanding of this appropriateness marks the educated person. Most types of word usage may be classified under the following headings: **archaic expressions, barbarisms, colloquialisms, improprieties, neologisms** (newly coined words), **provincialisms, slang, vulgarisms, hackneyed**, or **trite, expressions**, and **idiomatic expressions.**

655 **ARCHAIC EXPRESSIONS** Words are archaic that have become old-fashioned and no longer used naturally: *spirituous* (for *spirited*), *eftsoons* (for *soon after*), *methinks, avaunt.*

> ARCHAIC: The youthful crowd will be *convocated* here *anon.*
> MODERN: The young people will gather here soon.

656 **BARBARISMS** Word distortions, such as *alright, disremember, irregardless* are to be avoided in contemporary usage.

> BARBARISM: I *disremember* the incident.
> STANDARD: I do not remember the incident.

657 **COLLOQUIALISMS** Some expressions are correctly used in informal conversation or in informal writing that are not appropriate in formal composition. The ordinary contractions, such as *doesn't, hasn't,* and *can't,* are examples of colloquialisms. The modern colloquial style of writing requires great skill except when it reflects reported speech.

> COLLOQUIAL:*It's funny* that he *doesn't* return.
> FORMAL: It is strange that he does not return.

658 **IMPROPRIETIES** Good words may be used inappropriately, such as *set* for *sit, most* for *almost, accept* for *except, affect* for *effect:*

> IMPROPRIETY: It seems that *most all* the students are here.
> CORRECT: It seems that almost all the students are here.

659 **NEOLOGISMS** Large numbers of words are added to the language or changed in meaning each year, and they are not necessarily to be avoided. When in doubt, check with an up-to-date dictionary.

RECENTLY COINED: Many exciting developments can be expected from *gene-splicing* experiments.

That *bag lady* comes here to the park every day.

It takes only a few minutes to *blow-dry* my hair.

660 PROVINCIALISMS   Dialectal words, often nonstandard, are expressions used by local people and are peculiar to their region (province). Some examples are *carry* (for accompany), *poke* (for bag or sack), *cayuse* (for range horse), *jolt wagon* (for farm wagon).

PROVINCIAL: She cooked a meal in the *spider*.

GENERAL: She cooked a meal in the frying pan.

661 SLANG   Do you like new-looking jeans? Or do you want yours to look downright *scuzzy* before you can feel comfortable in them? Do you try to *ace out* in school? In some dictionaries *scuzzy* means "dirty or grimy." To *ace out* is to "get a high, perhaps the highest, mark in a class." Both terms are labeled slang and may already have disappeared from teenage language. Most slang is overworked and quickly worn to threads.

Slang may be the language of your group, but usually it would be wise not to use it in writing or in talking with older people. Adults may have at one time in their lives used a great deal of slang, but they know how tiresome and meaningless it may become. Still, slang is clever, forceful, or picturesque and may sometimes become part of the language of mature people—such words as *sob story, mob,* or *stooge* are now accepted. Slang should not be entirely despised, but it should be used with care.

Various terms are associated with slang in describing nonstandard usage: **dialect, patois, argot, jargon, cant, vernacular.** Each has its own particular application. See your dictionary.

662 VULGARISMS   Some words are never correct in either formal or informal expression: words such as *blowed, brung, busted* (for burst), *drawed, drownded, et, growed, hain't, hern, hisn, hisself, knowed, nowheres, scairt, theirn, theirselves, them there,* and *this here.* The term also applies to obscenities.

663 HACKNEYED, OR TRITE, EXPRESSIONS   Phrases that have been overused until they have almost lost their effectiveness are **trite.** Although young writers are tempted to use these worn-out expressions, or clichés, they should learn to substitute more vital ones. Some of the hackneyed terms frequently used are *brave as a lion, brown as a berry, busy as a bee, cold as ice, green as grass.*

664 Idiomatic Expressions   Idioms are expressions that are peculiar to a language. Since they often are not governed by the rules of its grammar, it is difficult to translate them into another language. Although idioms may defy analysis within the rules of grammar, they have nevertheless become, through long-continued usage, firmly established as standard.

That these expressions at first glance may not be parsed or diagrammed should not discourage their use. The very best writers of all languages make constant use of idioms. Some common English idioms are *put up with, all of a sudden, get rid of it, in the long run, get into hot water, with a grain of salt*. Be careful to use correct idioms. The prepositions especially are often determined by their idiomatic use rather than by logic:

UNIDIOMATIC: Hal *differed from* me about the movie.

CORRECT: Hal *differed with* me about the movie. (See 360.)

Usage Glossary

665 Some of the expressions listed here are in established use in **informal speech and writing**, but standard usage calls for the more **formal expression in writing**. Remember, however, that usage changes. Learn to check with the dictionary.

666 **Affect—effect.** *Affect* is a transitive verb meaning to *influence* or *to* means *to exclude* or *leave out*. As a preposition it means *but* or *excluding*.

I *accept* a gift.

We voted to *except* these members from service.

All the gifts *except* yours were returned.

Act. When used as a linking verb to mean "seem" or "pretend to be," *act* is followed by an adjective:

He certainly *acted* stupid.

Affect—effect. *Affect* is a transitive verb meaning *to influence* or *to pretend*. *Effect* as a verb means *to bring about; effect* as a noun means *result:*

The noise *affects* (not *effects*) my hearing.

They *effected* (not *affected*) a compromise.

His work had a good *effect* (not *affect*).

All right. Use the phrase *all right* rather than *alright;* the latter word is recorded but, as yet, with little approval for use.

Is it *all right* (not *alright*) to take the car?

Already—all ready. *Already* is the adverb:

The guests had come *already*.

We were *all ready* for the fun.

Alternative. This word means a *choice between two things*.

He had the *alternatives* of resigning or of being fired.

Altogether—all together. *Altogether* is the adverb:

This is *altogether* bad.

They were *all together* in the boat.

A one. It is archaic to use *a* with *one* in a sentence like this:

There was not *one* (not *a one*) who would volunteer.

As. After verbs of *saying, knowing, thinking,* or *feeling,* do not use *as* for *whether* or *that* (379).

I do not know *that* (not *as*) I can go.

So—as, as—as. In negative statements use the correlatives *so—as*; in positive statements use *as—as*:

He is not *so* tall *as* John.

He is *as* tall *as* John.

At. Do not use *at* unnecessarily with *where*:

Where is the book *at?* (Omit *at*.)

667 **Awful.** This term originally meant *awe-inspiring,* but it has been so weakened by its colloquial use that it can seldom be used in its original meaning. *Awful* and *awfully* should be avoided in most writing since they are merely general terms of emphasis or disapproval:

Jane is *unusually* (not *awfully*) smart.

This was a *difficult* (not an *awful*) job.

Badly. In formal writing do not use this adverb in the sense of *very much* nor as a predicate adjective (289):

I want *very much* (not *badly*) to succeed.

He looks *bad* (not *badly*) since his illness.

Compliment—complement. A compliment expresses *praise*; a complement *completes something*:

She paid him a sincere *compliment*.

The verb mentioned has two *complements*.

Considerable. Use this term as an adjective; rarely as a noun.

A *considerable* sum of money is invested in that plant.

They have done *considerable* for the school. (**informal**)

668 **Credible—credulous.** Credible means *believable*; credulous means *believing too easily*:

That is a *credible* story.

He was too *credulous* in accepting their account.

Disremember. This word is not standard though marked *colloquial* or *informal* in some dictionaries:

I do not *remember* (not I *disremember*) his name.

Either—neither. Best used to indicate one of two persons or things:

None (not *neither*) of the four boys would go.

Either of the *two* girls can take the part.

Neither of the *two* plans was approved.

669 Enthused. Although classed as colloquial by some dictionaries, it is shunned in good writing.

He is *enthusiastic* (not *enthused*) about the plan.

Expect. In formal writing do not confuse *expect*, meaning *to anticipate*, with *suppose*, meaning *to be of the opinion*:

I *suppose* (not *expect*) he is wealthy.

We *expect* to see you tomorrow.

Farther—further. The distinction between *farther* to refer to *spatial distance* and *further* to refer to *time, degree,* or *quantity* is increasingly observed by careful writers:

We walked *farther* than two miles.

I shall go no *further* with this business.

The explorer went *further* into the forest.

Fix. This is colloquial when used to mean *predicament, difficult situation,* or *condition* and badly overused:

I was in a desperate *situation* (not *fix*) about my grades.

Formally—formerly. *Formally* means *in a formal manner; formerly* means *previously*:

The guest was treated *formally*.

He was *formerly* mayor of the town.

Funny. Do not use for *odd* or *strange*, except in colloquial expressions:

It is *strange* (not *funny*) that he lost his fortune.

Gentleman—lady. These terms are sometimes applied to show respect but are more often merely pretentious. Of course, in addressing an audience the speaker still may correctly say: "Ladies and gentlemen." The terms *man* and *woman* are best for general use:

I met a pleasant woman (not *lady*) at the museum.

Get up. This two-word verb in the meaning of *organize, prepare,* or *arrange,* is now acceptable for general use though it is informal in feeling.

They *got up* a good party for the team.

670 Good. Do not use the adjective *good* as an adverb (329):

He sings *well* (not *good*).

Got. *Got,* with *had, has,* or *have* to indicate possession or obligation emphatically, is generally acceptable.

He *has got* the money here.

I *have got* to go immediately.

Had ought to. Do not use *had ought to* for *ought to* or *should:*

You *ought* (not *had ought*) to write to Ned.

You *should* (not *had ought to*) read this book.

Imply—infer. A speaker or writer may *imply* more than he says, the hearer *infers* what the speaker intends:

We *inferred* from what Jim said that he was angry with us.

The speaker did not *imply* that anyone in particular was to blame.

Invite—invitation. It is still dialectal, after three hundred years of use, to use the word *invite* for the noun *invitation:*

She has an *invitation* (not *invite*) to the lecture.

Is where—is when. These terms should not be used in definitions:

Subtraction is *taking* (not *where* or *when you take*) one number from another.

671 Kind of—sort of. It is still better (though opinion varies) not to use these terms for *rather* or *somewhat* (333).

He seems *rather* (not *sort of* or *kind of*) tired.

Lay—lie. *Lay* is usually transitive and takes a receiver of its action; its principal parts are *lay—laid—laid. Lie* is intransitive in its usual meanings and does not take an object; its principal parts are *lie—lay—lain* (but see 217).

Did you *lay* (not *lie*) the rake on the ground?

You should not *lie* (not *lay*) on the wet grass.

Learn—teach. To *learn* means to *get knowledge;* to *teach* means to *give knowledge* (227).

You should *learn* to play tennis.

Teach me how to swim.

Less—fewer. *Less* refers to *quantity; fewer* refers to *number:*

This lake has *less* water than the other.

This tree has *fewer* branches than that.

Liable—likely. *Likely* means *probably; liable* means *responsible* for or it may refer to a *possibility with unpleasant results:*

He is *likely* (not *liable*) to win the race.

He is *liable* for his own debts.

He is *liable* to harm someone.

Like. In formal writing do not use *like* for *as, as if,* or *as though,* in introducing a clause:

Do *as* (not *like*) I do.

He acted *as if* (not *like*) he knew it and *as though* (not *like*) he had always known it.

Mad. Do not use *mad* for *angry* in formal situations, though both are standard, for *mad* implies "insane" to many people.

John was *angry* (not *mad*) because of the delay.

Most. Do not use the adjective *most* for the adverb *almost* (316, 328); note also that *almost* is correct before indefinite pronouns: *almost* everybody, *almost* anyone:

We sold *almost* (not *most*) all the tickets.

672 Nohow. This adverb has been incorrectly used so long to create double negative constructions that, though it is standard in sense, it is best not to use it at all.

This machine won't run *at all* (not *nohow*).

None. This word has long been accepted as singular or plural:

None *were* pleased with the result.

None of the girls *was* present.

Off—from. Do not misuse *off* or *off of* for *from:*

He bought the book *from* (not *off* or *off of*) me.

Off of. The *of* is superfluous; when used it is informal.

He jumped *off* (not *off of*) the car.

Party. Do not use for *person* except in terms of law or in a jocular sense.

I saw the *person* (not *party*) who won the prize.

Raise—rear. Raise is now in good standard usage for "bring up" without distinction of kind, but the following distinctions have been made up to now.

They *reared* three children.

He *raised* hogs for market.

Raise—rise. In its usual meanings *raise* is transitive and takes a receiver of its action; its principal parts are *raise—raised—raised*. *Rise* is intransitive and almost never takes an object; its principal parts are *rise—rose—risen* (217):

Jim *raised* (not *rose*) the window.

The plane *rose* (not *raised*) quickly as it flew away.

673 Real. Avoid using the adjective *real* for the adverbs *very* or *really* (311).

She is *very* (not *real*) talented and *really* well educated.

His boat was in *real* (actual) danger.

Reason. A statement containing *the reason is* is preferably completed by a *that* clause:

The reason he succeeded is *that* (not *because*) he worked hard.

Reverend, Honorable. Do not place a surname immediately after either of these terms: *The Reverend George Smith, The Reverend Mr. Smith,* (not *Reverend Smith*); *The Honorable Susan Miller, The Honorable Mrs. Miller.*

Set—sit. *Set* is usually transitive and takes a receiver of its action; its principal parts are *set—set—set*. *Sit* is usually intransitive and does not take an object; its principal parts are *sit—sat—sat* (217):

Set (not *sit*) the chair in the corner.

We *sat* (not *set*) on the grass to rest.

So. Do not use it as an intensive in formal writing:

He is *extremely* (not *so*) careful.

674 Suspicion. It is not in good use as a verb:

They *suspected* (not *suspicioned*) him of theft.

This here—that there. Omit the dialectal *here* and *there*.

I like *this* (not *this here*) model and not *that* (not *that there*) one.

To—at. Do not use *to* for *at* in such sentences as this:

He is *at* (not *to*) home now.

Wait on. Do not use the dialectal *wait on* for *wait for*:

Do not *wait for* (not *wait on*) me if my plane is late.

Way—ways. Use the singular form in sentences like this:

He rode a short *way* (not *ways*) with us.

Widow woman. Omit *woman*:

She is a *widow* (not *widow woman*).

Wire. Should not be used for *telegram* in formal writing:

I will send you a *telegram* (not *wire*) tomorrow.

Without no. Do not use this double negative (336)

He worked without *any* (not *no*) plans.

Pronunciation

675 The only sure guide to correct pronunciation is a standard dictionary. The words listed here are some of those about whose pronunciation many people are uncertain. The words with a number are recorded as having two or three acceptable pronunciations. Other faults lie in stressing the wrong syllable or by adding an extra one. In some instances, long and short vowel sounds are confused. It is best to learn one correct form and stick to it.

abdomen [2]	coupon [2]	grimace [2]	library
acclimate [2]	creek [2]	harass [2]	literature [5]
admirable	defect [2]	hearth	maintenance
adult [2]	despicable [2]	height	mischievous
almond [3]	detail [2]	heinous	museum
apparatus [2]	docile [2]	horizon	paraffin
apricot [2]	encore [3]	hospitable [2]	penalize [2]
architect	exquisite [2]	idea [3]	pergola [2]
athlete	finance [3]	impious [2]	pumpkin [2]
automobile [3]	forehead [4]	impotent	quantity
bouquet [2]	formidable [3]	industry	recognize
chauffeur [2]	gape [2]	inquiry [4]	research [2]
chic	garage [3]	interesting [3]	sagacious [2]
cognomen [2]	genuine	irreparable	salmon
column	gondola [2]	irrevocable	surprise
combatant [2]	government [2]	Italian [2]	sword [2]
comparable	granary [2]	laboratory [3]	vagary [5]
condolence [2]	gratis [2]	lamentable [2]	villain

Figures of Speech

676 A **figure of speech** is a variation from the ordinary method of expression for the sake of effect. Though there are many figures of speech, the two in most common use are the **simile** and the **metaphor**. Others are **personification, hyperbole, metonymy,** and **synecdoche.** Figures of speech are employed effectively in both prose and poetry. Good examples of the use of the simile may be found in such familiar poems as Shelley's "To a Skylark" and Swenson's "Water Picture."

677 A **simile** is a direct comparison, introduced by *like* or *as*, of two things which in their general nature are different from each other:

She is *like a shining star*.   His hair is black *as* night.

678 A **metaphor** is implied comparison. Instead of stating the comparison, as in the simile, the likeness is suggested by terms not literally applicable to each other:

She is a *shining star*.   A *wave of emotion* overcame him.

679 Do not use mixed metaphors, such as these:

He is *aflame* with a *thirst* for knowledge.

Life is not all a rough *sea*; sometimes its *pathway* is smooth.

When a **simile** or a **metaphor** becomes involved and farfetched it is called a **conceit**.

680 **Personification** is the figure of speech in which some human char-acteristic is attributed to an inanimate thing:

The *friendly* hills seemed to *welcome* us.

681 **Hyperbole** is exaggeration for the purpose of emphasis and without any intention of being taken literally:

I am *completely starved.*

682 **Metonymy** is the substitution of the name of the whole for the name of the part, while **synecdoche** is the substitution of the part for the whole.

I am reading *Stevenson* (i.e., a book or poem by him).

This *camera* is broken (i.e., some part of it is broken).

They were stopped by a *badge* (i.e., someone with a badge, the police).

The ships dipped their *colors* (i.e., their flags).

Syllabication

683 Syllabication was originally a device of early printers to break words at the end of the printed line in order to give equal spacing between words and to keep the right margin aligned and parallel with the left margin. In general, the division in printed form follows the syllables of the spoken language. But, as there are so many exceptions due to the variations in the spelling and derivation of English words, the only sure guide to ascertain the correct current use is to refer to a good dictionary rather than to rely on one's ear.

EXAMPLE: syl-lab-i-ca-tion (spelled). si-lab-i-ca-tion (pronounced). The following rules should be followed in handwriting and typing:

1. Never divide words pronounced as one syllable: *drowned.*

2. Never divide words of two syllables with one a single vowel: *even, over.*

3. Do not divide the parts of a name: *John Smith, Mr. Jones.*

4. Do not divide numbers or abbreviations: *10,000, C.O.D., SOS.*

5. Do not divide endings such as: *-tial, -tion, -cious, -geous.*

6. Do not separate a final syllable of one or two letters: *-a, -ed, -es.*

7. Do not divide hyphened compounds except at the hyphen: *all-around, all- around.*

Spelling—Words Often Confused

684   English, like other languages, has a number of paired words that
cause confusion. There are four classes of such words.

1. **Homonyms.** These words are identical in spelling and pronunciation, but they differ in origin and meaning:

> *butter*, food; *butter*, one who butts
> *pool*, water; *pool*, the game

2. **Homophones.** These words are identical in pronunciation, but
they differ in origin, spelling, and meaning:

> *fair*, market; *fare*, food and drink; *fare*, tariff
> *red*, color; *read*, past tense of *read*

3. **Homographs.** These words are identical in spelling, but they differ
in origin, meaning, and sometimes in pronunciation:

> *fair*, market; *fair*, beautiful
> *wind*, air current; *wind*, to coil

4. **Heteronyms.** These words are identical in spelling, but they differ
in origin, pronunciation, and meaning:

> *bass*, fish; *bass*, male voice, musical term
> *row*, a line; *row*, a fight

♦ Sometimes **homographs** that are in the pattern of *fair* in Number 3
are loosely classified as **homonyms**.

♦ Words such as "head" in English, "tête" in French, "cabeza" in
Spanish, are true **synonyms** when used in their literal meaning—in
these illustrations, anatomical.

Here are homophones which everyone should be able to spell and
define correctly (in English there are at least three hundred seventy-
five such paired word groups):

aisle—isle	beach—beech	canvas—canvass
all—awl	beat—beet	capital—capitol
altar—alter	beau—bow	ceiling—sealing
ant—aunt	been—bin	cell—sell
arc—ark	bell—belle	cellar—seller
ascent—assent	berth—birth	cent—sent—scent
ate—eight	bier—beer	cereal—serial
aught—ought	blew—blue	choir—quire
bail—bale	board—bored	chord—cord
bait—bate	born—borne	clause—claws
ball—bawl	bough—bow	coarse—course
bare—bear	brake—break	council—counsel
base—bass	buy—by	creak—creek
be—bee	calendar—calender	currant—current

dear—deer
dew—due
die—dye
done—dun
earn—urn
fain—feign
faint—feint
fair—fare
feat—feet
fir—fur
flea—flee
flew—flue
flour—flower
fore—four
foul—fowl
freeze—frieze
gait—gate
great—grate
groan—grown
guest—guessed
hair—hare
hale—hail
hall—haul
hart—heart
heal—heel
hear—here
heard—herd
heir—air
hew—hue
hoes—hose
hole—whole
holy—wholly
hour—our
idol—idle
in—inn
jam—jamb
kernel—colonel
knead—need
knew—new
knot—not
know—no
lain—lane
lead—led

lessen—lesson
lie—lye
load—lode
loan—lone
made—maid
mail—male
main—mane
manner—manor
mantel—mantle
meat—meet
medal—meddle
might—mite
miner—minor
moan—mown
muscle—mussel
night—knight
none—nun
one—won
pail—pale
pain—pane
pause—paws
pair—pare—pear
peace—piece
peal—peel
plain—plane
pore—pour
pray—prey
pride—pried
principal—principle
profit—prophet
rain—rein—reign
raise—raze
read—reed
read—red
real—reel
rest—wrest
rhyme—rime
right—write—wright—rite
ring—wring
road—rode—rowed
role—roll
rose—rows
rough—ruff

rye—wry
sail—sale
scene—seen
sea—see
seam—seem
seine—sane
sew—sow—so
shone—shown
sight—site—cite
slay—sleigh
sleight—slight
slew—slue—slough
soar—sore
sole—soul
some—sum
son—sun
staid—stayed
stair—stare
stake—steak
stationary—stationery
steal—steel
stile—style
straight—strait
suite—sweet
tail—tale
their—there
threw—through
throne—thrown
to—too—two
toe—tow
vail—veil—vale
vain—vane—vein
vice—vise
wade—weighed
waist—waste
wait—weight
ware—wear
warn—worn
wave—waive
way—weigh
week—weak
whole—hole
wood—would

Spelling

685 THE WRITTEN WORD An essential characteristic of good writing is correct spelling. American English in its written form was initially recorded in Samuel Johnson's first American dictionary published in New Haven, Connecticut, in 1798. This Samuel Johnson was not related to Doctor Samuel Johnson, the sage of Fleet Street, whose famous English dictionary was published in London in 1755.

In the American Johnson's work, the beginnings of simplified spelling first appeared, later to be amplified in Noah Webster's *American Dictionary* of 1828. There is for the English language no authoritative arbiter of usage such as the *Académie Française* or the *Accademia della Crusa* of France and Italy "to sift the husks and purify the language." In general, dictionaries of the English language rely on recording the language as it is "used" rather than "how it ought to be." It is inevitable then that different dictionaries will reflect the tastes of different times, different places, and different lexicographers. Nevertheless, there is such a wide area of agreement in our standard American English spelling that a misspelled word is inexcusable.

Spelling List and Vocabulary Builder

The words in this list should be learned and mastered as they comprise a working vocabulary of high frequency and usefulness. Most of these words are among those frequently misspelled by writers and printers alike. At times, it is a matter of confusing words very similar in form: conf*ident* (adjective) and conf*idant* (noun). Again, such words as *elicit* and *illicit* are often used in error because of a partial similarity in sound. The suffixes *-able* and *-ible* are not always correctly distinguished.

The homophones, in section 684, are not repeated in this list. They should be added to the list as a genuine part of a good vocabulary. To illustrate, consider this EXAMPLE: An important spelling error may occur, when we permit the "advice" of *counsel* to "advise" us to speak out in the *council*, although we were ruled out of order by the council chairperson.

The principal parts of irregular verbs, in section 204, are to be considered as a part of this spelling list and should be learned for both their correct use and their spelling in writing. EXAMPLE: Now that I *know* him—and *knowing* him as well as I do—I *knew* that I should have *known* all about him before this.

The word list, in section 675, on developing dictionary skills, provides another group that includes forty-nine words not appearing in this section.

♦ Note that, in this listing, the dictionary style of entry for run-in words is used: thus, *agree, -able, -ment* is to be read as *agree, agreeable, agreement*. Note also that *-ing* or *-d* or *-ed*, is used to indicate an adjective formed on a noun or verb base rather than the participle, present or past form, or a part of a **verb phrase** (41, 181).

abattoir
abhor, –rence
abhorrent
ability
absence
absolute, –ly
absorb, –able,
    –ing
absorption
abundance
abundant, –ly
accede
accelerate, –d
acceleration
accept, –ed,
    –ance
access, –ible
accident, –al,
    –ally
accommodate
accommodation
accompanist
accompany, –ing
accomplice
accomplish, –ed,
    –ment
accord, –ance
account, –ing
accumulate, –d
accurate, –ly
accustom, –ed
ache
achieve, –ment
acknowledge, –d
acknowledgment
acquaint, –ance
acquire, –d
across
actual, –ly
adapt, –able,
    –ability
addition, –al
address, –ed, –ee
admissible
admit, –tance
advantage, –ous
advertise, –d,
    –ment

advertising
advice
advise, –ment
aerial
aeronautics
affect, –ed, –ing
affection, –ate,
    –ately
affidavit
against
aggravate, –d
aggravation
aggressive, –ly
aghast
agree, –d, –able,
    –ment
agricultural
agriculture
alcohol, –ic
allow, –ed, –ance
all right
already
although
altogether
aluminum
always
amateur, –ish
ammonia
among
amount
amuse, –d,
    –ment
analogous
analysis
analyze
ancient, –ly
angle, –d
anniversary
announce, –d,
    –ment
annual, –ly
answer
antenna
anticipate, –d
anticipation
anxiety
anxious, –ly,
    –ness

apologize
apology
apparatus
apparent, –ly
appeal, –ed,
    –able, –ing
appear, –ance
appetite
application
apply
appoint, –ed,
    –ive
appreciate, –d
appreciative, –ly
approach, –ed,
    –able
approximate, –d,
appropriation
approval
approve, –d,
approximate, –d,
    –ly
aquanaut
arbitrary, –ly
arctic
argue
arguing
argument
arrange, –d,
    –ment
article
artificial
ascend, –able
ascendant
ascertain, –ed,
    –able
assassin, –ate,
    –ated
assiduous, –ly
assign, –ed, –able,
    –ment
assist, –ed, –ance
association
assume, –d
assurance
astronaut
athlete

athletic
attach, –ed, –able
attack, –ed, –able
attempt, –ed
attend, –ed,
      –ance
attention
attitude
attorney
attract, –ed, –ive,
      –ively
audience
authoritative, –ly
authority
automobile
autumn, –al
auxiliary
avail, –able, –ing
average, –d
aviation
awful, –ly
awkward, –ly
backslide
baggage
balance, –d
ballet
ballistics
balloon
ballot
bandage, –d
banquet
banquette
bargain, –ed
barrel, –led
base, –ment
basis
battalion
becoming, –ly
beggar, –ed
beginning
behavior, –al
belief
believe, –r
belligerent, –ly
beneficent
beneficial, –ly
beneficiary
benefit, –ed

bicycle, –d
biscuit
blizzard
bookkeeping
boundary
breadth
breath
breathe, –d
brief, –ly
brilliant, –ly
broad, –ly
bruise, –d
budget, –ed
bulletin
buoyant, –ly
bureau, –crat
burglar, –ize
bury
business, –like
busy, –ness
cabin
cafeteria
campaign, –er
cancel, –ed
candidate
canoe
capacity
captain
career
careless, –ness
carriage
carrier
carry, –ing
cashier, –d
categorical, –ly
category
caution, –ed,
      –ary
celebrate, –d
celebration
cemetery
century
certain, –ly
certificate
certification
changeable
character, –ize
chauffeur

chemistry
chief, –tain
chocolate
choice
choose
chose, –n
circular, –ize
civilization
climate
climb, –ed
clothe, –s
clothing
coach, –ed
coalesce, –d
coherent, –ly
collar
college
collegiate
color, –ful
colossus
column
coming
commence
commercial, –ly
commission, –ed,
      –er
committee, –man,
      –woman
communicate, –d
community
comparative, –ly
comparison
compel, –led
competent, –ly
competition
complain
complement,
      –ary
complexion, –ed
compliment, –ed,
      –ary
computer, –ize
concede, –d
conceive, –d
concern, –ed,
      –ing
concert, –ed
concession

conclude, –d

concrete, –ly

condemn, –ed

condition, –ed,
    –al

confection, –er,
    –ery

confer, –red,
    –ring

conference

confidant

confidence

confident, –ial,
    –ly

congratulate

congratulation

connoisseur

consensus

conscience

conscientious

consequence

consequent, –ial

considerable

considerably

consistent, –ly

constitution, –al

contempt, –ible

continual, –ly

continue, –d

control, –led,
    –ling, –lable

controversial

convenient

convenience

convince, –d

cool, –ly

co-op

cooperate, –d

cordial, –ly

corduroy

corespondent

corporation

correspond, –ed,
    –ent, –ence

cough

couldn't

country

county

courage, –ous

courteous, –ly

courtesy

cousin

credence

critic, –ism

cruel, –ly

curiosity

curriculum

curtain

custom, –er
    –ary

cylinder

daily

decease, –d

deceive, –d

decide

decision

decisive

declaration

decorate, –d

decorative

defense

defensive

definite, –ly

definition

definitive, –ly

delicious, –ly

delirious

depend, –ant,
    –ent, –ency

depot

descend, –ed,
    –ant, –ent

describe, –d

description

descriptive, –ly

desert, –ed

deserts

deserve, –d

design, –ing

desirous

desperate, –ly

dessert

determine, –d

develop, –ed,
    –ment

diamond

dictionary

didn't

difference

different, –ly

difficult, –y

dilapidated

diminish, –ed

diphtheria

diploma

diplomat

direct, –ly, –or

disagree, –able,
    –ment

disappear, –ance,
    –ed

disappoint, –ed,
    –ment

disapprove, –d

disaster

disastrous, –ly

discipline, –d

discover, –ed,
    –able

discuss, –ed,
    –ion, –ible

disease, –d

dissipate, –d

distinguish, –ed,
    –able

distribute, –d

distribution

divide, –d

divine

divisible

division, –al

doctor

dominant

don't

doubt, –ed

dual

duchess

duel

duly

duplicate, –d

duplication

during

dyeing

dying

earnest, –ly,
 —ness
easily
easy
economic, –s, –al
economy
ecstacy
effect, –ive, –ual
effervescent
efficiency
efficient, –ly
eighth
either
elaborate, –d,
 –ly, –ness
electric, –ity, –al
electronic, –s
elephant
elevator
elicit, –ed
eligible
eliminate, –d
embarrass, –ing,
 —ment
emerge, –d, –ncy
emphasis
emphasize, –d
employ, –ed, –er,
 –ee, –able,
 —ment
encourage, –d,
 —ment
encyclopedia
endeavor
endorse, –ment
enemy
engineer, –ing
enormous, –ly
enough
entertain, –ed,
 –er, –ment
enthusiast, –ic
entrance
envelope
envelopment
environment, –al
equip, –ped,
 —ment

equivalence
equivalent
equivocal
ere, e're
especially
essential, –ly
establish, –ed,
 —ment
every
evidence
exaggerate, –d
exaggeration
exceed, –ed
excellent, –ly
excellence
except, –ed
 –ion, –ing
excess, –ive,
 –ively
excite, –d, –dly,
 —ment
executive
exercise, –d
exhibit, –ed,
 –ion
exhilarating
exhort, –ation
existence
existent
exorbitant, –ly
expedition, –ary
expensive, –ly
experience, –d
explain, –ed
explanation
explicit, –ly
express, –ed, –ly,
 –ion
expressive, –ness
exquisite, –ly
extend, –ed, –ible
extension
extinct, –ion
extreme, –ly
facilitate, –d
fallacy
familiar
famous, –ly

fascinate, –d
fascinating
fashion, –ed,
 –able
fatigue, –d
fatiguing
faucet
favorite
feature, –d
February
federal
fertile
fictitious
field
fierce
fiery (fire)
filth, –y, –iness
final, –ly
finance
financial, –ly
flight
flourish, –ing
foreign, –er
foreword
formally
formerly
fortunate, –ly
forty
forward
fountain, –head
fourth
freight
friend, –ly,
 –liness
fulfill, –ed,
 —ment
fundamental, –ly
gage
garage
gardener
gasoline
gauge
general, –ly
generosity
generous, –ness
genius
genuine, –ly,
 –ness

geographic, –al
geography
ghastly
glorious, –ly
government, –al
governor
gracious, –ly
gradation
graduation
grammar
grandeur
grateful, –ly
gratitude
grease
great, –ly
grief
grievous, –ly
grocery
guarantee, –d
guard, –ed
guardian, –ship
guide, –d
guilt, –y, –ily,
    –inesss
guttural, –ly
gymnasium
hammer, –ed
handkerchief
handle, –d
handsome, –ly
hansom (cab)
happen, –ing
happiness
harass, –ment
harbor
hardiness
hardness
haste
hastily
height
heretofore
herringbone
hesitate
hesitation
heyday
hinder, –ing
hindrance
Hippocratic
    (oath)

historic, –al
history
holiday
honor, –ed,
    –able
horrible, –ness
horrid, –ly, –ness
hospitable
hospital, –ity,
    –ize,
    –ization
human, –e
humor, –less,
    –ous
hundred
hundredth
hungry
hurricane
hydrogen
hymn, –al
hypercritical
hypocrisy
hypocrite
hypocritical
idea
identified
identify
identity
ignorance
illiteracy
illiterate
illustrate, –d
illustration
imagination
imagined
imitation
immediate, –ly
immense, –ly
immortal, –ity
impatience
impatient, –ly
impedance
import, –ed, –ant,
    –antly,
    –ance,
    –ation
impossible
impresario

improve, –d,
    –ment
incessant, –ly
incidence
incident, –al, –ally
incinerate
incompatibility
incompatible
inconvenience
inconvenient, –ly
incorrigible
incredible
independent, –ly
indict, –ment
indispensable
individual, –ly
industrial
industrious, –ness
inevitable, –ness
inferior, –ity
influence
influential
ingenious
ingenuous
inimitable
innocent
innocuous
inoculate
inoculation
instance, –d
instant, –aneous,
    –ly
instead
institute
institution, –al
insurance
intelligence
intelligent, –ly
interest, –ing,
    –ingly
interfere, –nce
interpret, –ation
interrupt, –ed, –er
interview, –er,
    –ed, –ing
intimate, –ly
invalid

invalid, –ate,
    –ated
invariably
investigate, –d
investigation
invitation
invite, –d
invoice
irrelevant
irreparable
irresistible
irrigate
irrigation
island
issue, –d
jackknife
jaguar
janitor
jargon
jaundice, –d
jealous, –y
jewelry
journal, –ism
journey
judgment
juicy
justice
kitchen
khaki
kindergarten
knickknack
knowledgeable
knowledge
label, –ed
laboratory
language
later
latter
laugh
laundry
lawyer
league
lecture
leeway
legal, –ity, –ize
legislate
legislature
leisure, –ly

length
lettuce
liability
liable
librarian
library
license, –d
lieutenant
lighten, –ing, –ed
lightning
likely
linoleum
liquefy
liquefiable
liquid, –ate,
    –ation
liquor
listen, –er, –able
literary
literate
literature
liveliest
livelihood
lively
living
lodgment
loneliness
lonely
loose, –ly, –ned
lose, –r
losing
lovable
love, –ly, –liness
lunch, –eon
machine, –d
magazine
magnificent, –ly
maintain
maintenance
majority
mammoth
manage, –able
    –ment
manifold
manufactory
manufacture, –d,
    –r
manyfold

marriage
marry, –ing
material, –ly
matériel
maternity
mathematics
mattress
mayor, –alty
measure, –d
medicinal
medicine
medium
mercenary
merchandise
merchantman
merit, –ed
message
metal, –lic
mettle, –some
mileage
millionaire
miniature
minimum
minute
mirror, –ed
miscellaneous
mischief
mischievous
miser, –ly
miserable
misery
missionary
missile
misspell, –ed
    –ing
moccasin
moist, –ure,
    –urize
momentous
monument, –al
moral, –ly
morale
mortgage, –d
mountainous
murmur
musician, –ly
mutilate, –d
myth, –ical

mythology
nadir
naphtha
narrate
narrative
natural, –ly
nautical
naval
navel
navigating
navigation, –al
necessary
necessity
nickel
niece
nihilism
nineteen, –th
ninetieth
ninety
nonsense
notice, –able
notwithstanding
nowadays
nuclear
nuisance
obbligato
obdurate
occasion
occur, –red,
   –rence
octopus
oculist
ominous, –ly
omission
omit, –ted
onerous
operate
operating
opinion, –ated
opportunity
opposite
opposition
oppress, –ed, –ive,
   –or
optician
optimism
optimistic
oratorio
oratory

orchestra, –l
origin, –al, –ality
oxygen
pamphlet
paragraph
parallel, –ism
paralysis
paralyze
paraphernalia
parenthesis
parliament, –ary
participial
participle
particular, –ize,
   –ly
passed
pastime
pastor
paternity
pavilion
peasant
peculiar, –ly
penance
pendulum
penguin
peninsula, –r
penitent, –ial,
   –iary
perforation
perform, –ance
perhaps
permanent, –ly
permissible
permissive, –ness
perseverance
persist, –ent,
   –ence
person, –al, –able,
   –ality, –alty
personnel
perspiration
persuade, –r
persuasion
pertain, –ing
pervade
phenomenal, –ly
Philippines
philosophic, –al
philosophy

physical
physician
physicist
physics
picnic, –king
plain, –ly
plan, –ned
plane
plaque
plastic, –s
pleasant, –ly,
   –ness
pneumonia
poison, –er, –ous
ponderous, –ly
possession
possibility
possible
practical, –ly, –ity
practice
precede, –nce
precious
prefer, –red,
   –ence,
   –ential
preform, –ed
prejudice, –d
preparation
prepare
preservation
preserve, –d
prevalent, –ly
preventive
prison, –er
privilege, –d
probable
probably
procedure
proceed, –ing
profess, –or
proffer, –ed
prominent
promontory
pronounce, –d
pronunciation
propel, –ler
prophecy
prophesy
psychiatry

psychology
pumpkin
pursue, –r
pursuit
quaking
qualified
qualify
quandary
quarantine
quarrel
quarter, –ed
questionnaire
quiescent
quiet, –ed, –ly
quite
quorum
quote
quoth
radar
radiant, –ly
radiation
radiator
real, –ly
realize
rebut, –tal
recede
receipt, –ed
receive, –d
receptacle
reciprocal, –ly
reclaim, –ed
reclamation
recognition
recognize, –d
recommend, –ed,
    –ation
redundant
refer, –red, –ence
refrigerator
rehabilitation
relevance
relevant, –ly
relieve
religious, –ly
reluctance
reluctant, –ly
remembrance
renegade
reparation

repetition
represent, –ation,
    –ative
rescind
reservoir
respect, –ed, –ful,
    –fully
responsibility
restaurant
rheumatism
rhythm, –ic, –ical
ridiculous, –ly
roommate
rummage
sabbath
sacrament
sacrifice
sacrilegious
sagacious
sail, –ing, –er, –or
salary
sandwich
sanitary
satellite
satire
satisfaction
satisfactory
scarcity
schedule, –d
science
scientific
scissors
secretary
seize, –d
seminary
separate, –d, –ly
sergeant
several, –ly
shepherd, –ess
shining
shoulder
shrubbery
siege
significant, –ly
silhouette
similar, –ly
simultaneous, –ly
since
sincere, –ly

ski, –ing
slimmest
sociable
social
solemn, –ity
sophomore
source
sovereign, –ty
spaceship
sparsely
specie
species
specific
specimen
speech
sphere
statue
stature
statute
straight, –en
straitjacket
stratagem
strategy
strenuous, –ly
stretch, –able,
    –ability
stubborn, –ness
studying
subtle
suburban
succeed, –ing
success, –ive,
    –ively
sufficient, –ly
suffrage
sugar
suit, –able,
    –ability
summary
superficial, –ly
superintend, –ent
supersede
suppress, –ed,
    –ion
surprise, –d
surround, –ed,
    –ing
syllable
symmetrical

symmetry	tranquil, –lity	view, –ing
synonym, –ous	transfer, –red,	vilify
system, –atic,	–rence	villain
–atically	transistor, –ize	visible
tacit	treasure, –d, –r	visit, –or, –ation
tariff	truculent	vitamin
technical, –ly	true, –ness	vocation
technique	truly	voice, –d
telegram	truth	volume
temperament	tying	voluble
temperature	typical, –ly	waggish
temporarily	typography	wander, –ing,
temporary	tyrannical, –ly	–lust
tend, –ency	unanimous, –ly	warrant, –ee, or,
terrible	undoubted, –ly	–y
territorial	universal, –ly	weather, –ed
territory	university	Wednesday
theater	unmistakable	weight
theatrical, –ly	unnecessary	weird, –ness
therefore	upper, –most	whether
they, –'re	use, –d, –ful, –less	which
thief	usual, –ly	whom
thievery	usurious	whose
thorough, –ly,	utter, –ance	width
–ness	vacation	witch
though	vaccination	withhold
thousandths	vacillate	won't
tire, –d, –less,	vacillation	worst
–dness	valuable	wouldn't
tobacco	variety	writing
toboggoning	various	yacht
together	vegetable	yearn
tongue	vehicle	yeoman
topography	velocity	yield
tortuous	vengeance	you're
torturous	vertical, –ly	zeal, –ous, –ously
touch, –ing, –able	vicinity	zenith
tragedy	victuals	

686 The Dictionary as a Tool   One of the areas of difference in usage is, of course, the spelling of the words and forms of the written language. The young writer will find that the best tool for controlling this aspect of expression is a dictionary. Its constant use is a *must*. A dictionary verifies one's spelling when there is doubt; where more than one form is acceptable, it records them in one place; when certain spellings have restricted application, it states the fact; and when regional differences affect the choice of form (American vs. British, standard vs. dialectal, serious vs. humorous, for example), a dictionary indicates the preference.

Compounding

687 English compound words give much spelling trouble to writers everywhere, because there are so many of them. Here is an area where the "rules" applicable are often at variance with actual usage. Memorize as many as you can. In fact, several books detailing the technique have been written about the compounding of English words. Note these few illustrative examples of the large number of patterns possible:

airplane	= noun + noun
press agent	= noun (used as adjective) + noun
spoilsport	= verb + noun
good-looking	= adjective + participle
uptown	= adverb + noun
newlywed	= adverb + participle
newly wed couple	= adverb + participle + noun
old-age pension	= adjective + noun + noun
Mexican-American	= proper adjective + proper adjective

What is an English compound word? It is the combination of several standard words which, when used together, create a new concept of meaning. Thus, every *black bird* is not necessarily a *blackbird*; a *workingman* does not mean a *man* is *working*; a *storeroom* does not mean a *room* in a *store*; a *cornflower* is not the *flower* of the *corn* plant. Each compound, then, becomes a word in its own right.

There are three types of compounds to be considered: (1) The solid form, *outlaw, textbook*, (to) *shortchange*; (2) the hyphenated form, *X-ray, city-state, well-known*; (3) the word-phrase form of two or more words, *red tape, printing press, post office*. Your dictionary is the proper source for determining what is the actual and correct form to be used in writing, especially since some compounds may vary their form depending on their function in a sentence. X-ray is hyphenated as a verb, for example, but not as a noun. *Well-known* is hyphenated as an attributive adjective but not when it is used after a linking verb. Once you have chosen the correct form, always be consistent in using it.

688 **THE UNIT MODIFIER** This hyphened form is a conventional, recorded two-noun phrase or an improvised literal compound adjective that is used only before a noun:

cast iron   – a *cast-iron* bridge
gas meter – a *gas-meter* reading
folk dance – a *folk-dance* festival
rush hour – a *rush-hour* crush
           – an *ever-winding* road
           – an *always-smoking* chimney
           – a *reddish-brown* paint
           – an *off-and-on* game
           – a *tongue-in-cheek* remark

About Words

689 FOREIGN WORDS AND PHRASES This class of words must be carefully checked as to spelling, including accent marks, and as to whether they are or are not considered anglicized; that is, whether they should be italicized as foreign words or phrases:

auf Wiedersehen   – German
au jus   – French
amok   – Malayan
flora   – New Latin: Flora
Córdoba   – Spanish: *Cordova*
Van Gogh [van go]   – Dutch: *vän Khokh*
habeas corpus   – Medieval Latin (you may have the person)

690 MISSPELLING AS AN "ART FORM."

The Duk iz a kind ov short legged hen.
They kan sale on the water as natral and eazy as a grease spot.
Duks hav a broad bill which enables them tew eat their food without anny spoon.
There aint any room on the outside of a Duk for enny more feathers.
The duk don't kro like a rooster, but quaks like a duk.

—JOSH BILLINGS (Henry W. Shaw) 1818–1885

691 VOCABULARY The ability to express one's thoughts and to understand the expression of the thoughts of others can be measured by one's knowledge of the meaning of words. A good and expressive vocabulary is, obviously, an invaluable aid to success in any field. It must include the words in the vocabularies of the student's special fields of interest—be it art, music, engineering, agriculture, space science, or ecology—with their **synonyms** (words of the same general meaning but different in their specific application) and **antonyms** (words of opposite meaning).

692 THE USE OF A DICTIONARY The use of a standard unabridged dictionary is valuable in building a vocabulary. It gives extensive information about every word—pronunciation, part of speech (38), derivation, illustrations of current usage, various meanings, synonyms, and antonyms. In a section, usually at the front of the dictionary, all the symbols used in its pronunciation system are explained, and the diacritical marks are fully illustrated.

693 A PLAN FOR VOCABULARY BUILDING To develop a good, working vocabulary requires time, patience, and persistence. One good plan is to write in a notebook all unfamiliar words that one reads or hears. Unfamiliar words and word uses found in reading one's own books should be marked so that the meaning may be studied in context (696). A periodic review of what has been noted reinforces learning.

694 VOCABULARY AND VERSE Through the writing of rhymed verse (564–568), one may enlarge one's vocabulary, because words must be selected for meaning as well as for sound. The sonnet (573, 574) is a good stanza form to use because of its rigid rhyme requirements. The limerick (576) is also a good form, which may be used in either light or serious mood. Writing parodies (imitations) of popular verse is not only fun but also a profitable exercise in word substitution. Specimens of these types of writing are to be found in current newspapers and magazines. The improvised limerick and sonnet below suggest possibilities:

SUCCESS

You think you are well on your way,
Assured you make progress each day;
Yet, nevertheless,
Your final success
Depends on the words that you say.

WORDS

The words we use may be but stumbling blocks
To make more arduous our upward way—
Along our path but rough, projecting rocks
To bruise our weary feet from day to day;
And yet, it's folly we are thus oppressed,
For words may help us on to higher things:
One who with mastery of words is blest
Not only upward toils, but starward goes on wings.
Unwise are they who fail to count the cost
Of clumsy, careless words that flout success,
But wisdom theirs who see as won or lost
Through use of words life's greatest happiness.
He who for artistry in language strives
Finds rich return: with words we shape our lives.

695 SPECIAL-SUBJECT DICTIONARIES AND GLOSSARIES   Almost every area of knowledge today has its own special vocabulary of words and terms. Sometimes, specialized words are included as a part of a book on a given subject to show how the author has used them in developing the subject. At times the use may differ, in some limiting aspect, from the standard definition of a word or phrase. A compilation of such word-usage is called a **glossary**. It may be included within a book as an appendix, or it may be extensive enough to be issued as a separate book or pamphlet.

In vocabulary building, such dictionaries and glossaries should not be overlooked, for they are a rich source of specialized information.

696 WORDS IN CONTEXT   *Context* comes from Latin words meaning "the weaving together of words." In its modern definition, it refers to the parts surrounding a word or a sentence that influence its meaning. One can often guess the meaning of an unfamiliar word by studying its context.

Thus, the association of words with each other is important in vocabulary building. To illustrate, consider the word *eye*, the organ of vision in animals. By various figures of speech we have: a *black* eye (area); *brown* eye (color of the iris of the eye); keep an *eye* on (watch carefully); cast an *eye* over (look at); in the public *eye* (in the presence of); an evil *eye* (particular expression of); an *eye* for girls (interest in); the *eye* of the riot (focal point); the *eye* of the storm (central area); electric *eye* (in resemblance to the human eye); *eye* of the wind (direction); *eye* to *eye* (in agreement with).

Using the Library

697 THE LIBRARY   Many libraries now use the Dewey Decimal System or the Library of Congress classification system. The Dewey system classifies all works exclusive of fiction into ten major groups and each group further into ten subgroups. Following is a simple description of the major groups:

000–099	General works, such as encyclopedias
100–199	Philosophy, psychology
200–299	Religion, mythology
300–399	Social sciences, such as government, sociology, economics, and books on clubs, holidays, and etiquette
400–499	Languages: grammar, linguistics
500–599	Pure science: mathematics, physics, chemistry, botany, zoology, earth science, biological sciences

600–699   Applied science: inventions, gardening, cooking, sewing, aeronautics, engineering, medicine, agriculture

700–799   Arts and recreation: drawing, painting, music, sports

800–899   Literature (except fiction)

900–999   History: travel, geography, biography

Certain books may not be shelved according to their class number.

1. Short-story collections may be marked SC and shelved separately. They are arranged alphabetically by the last name of the editor.

2. Books of biography are shelved according to the last name of the person they are about. Some libraries use the Dewey Decimal number 921, many prefer 92, and some use only the letter B to indicate biography. Below either 921, 92, or B on the catalogue card is the initial of the person written about.

3. Reference books like encyclopedias and atlases are usually shelved together. The letter R above the number indicates a reference book.

4. Fiction is shelved separately. Books of fiction are arranged alphabetically by the last name of the author.

More precise in its ability to classify books is the Library of Congress classification system, in which a set of capital letters is combined with numbers. A broad area, such as literature, is indicated by a letter. A subdivision of that area is shown by a second capital letter, and further subdivisions are shown by numbers.

Bibliography

Grammar, Usage, Linguistics, and the Teaching of English

Barzun, Jacques. *Simple and Direct: A Rhetoric for Writers*. Revised edition. New York: Harper & Row, Publishers, 1984.

Baugh, Albert C. and Thomas Cable. *A History of the English Language*. Third edition. New York: Prentice-Hall, 1978.

Bernstein, Theodore. *The Careful-Writer: A Modern Guide to English Usage*. New York: Atheneum Publishers, 1965.

———. *Miss Thistlebottom's Hobgoblins*. New York: Simon and Schuster, 1984.

Bryant, Margaret M., ed. *Current American Usage: How Americans Say It and Write It*. New York: T. Y. Crowell, 1965.

Claiborne, Robert. *Our Marvelous Native Tongue: The Life and Times of the English Language*. New York: Times Books, 1983.

Curme, George O. *English Grammer*. New York: Barnes & Noble, Inc. (College Outline Series), 1947.

———. *A Grammar of the English Language*: Vol. I, *Parts of Speech*; Vol. 2, *Syntax*. Essex, Conn.: Verbatim Books, 1983.

Ebbitt, Wilma R. and David R. Ebbitt. *Writer's Guide and Index to English*. Seventh edition. Glenview, Ill.: Scott, Foresman & Co., 1982.

Evans, Bergen, and Cornelia Evans. *A Dictionary of Contemporary American Usage*. New York: Random House, 1957.

Follett, Wilson. *Modern American Usage; A Guide*. Edited and completed by Jacques Barzun and others. New York: Hill & Wang, 1966.

Fowler, Henry W. *A Dictionary of Modern English Usage*. Second edition, revised and edited by Sir Ernest Gowers. Oxford: Oxford University Press, 1983.

Gleason, H. A., Jr. *Linguistics and English Grammar*. New York: Holt, Rinehart and Winston, Inc., 1965.

Jesperson, Otto. *Growth and Structure of the English Language*. Tenth edition. Chicago: University of Chicago Press, 1982.

Laird, Charlton. *The Word: A Look at the Vocabulary of English*. New York: Simon and Schuster, 1981.

Lazarus, Arnold, and Wendell Smith. *Glossary of Literature and Composition*. Revised edition. Urbana, Ill.: National Council of Teachers of English, 1983.

Newman, Edwin. *Strictly Speaking*. New York: Warner Books, 1975.

Partridge, Eric. *Usage and Abusage: A Guide to Good English*. Baltimore, Md.: Penguin Books, 1963.

Roberts, Paul. *Understanding Grammar*. New York: Harper & Row, Publishers, Inc., 1954.

Sapir, Edward. *Language: An Introduction to the Study of Speech*. Orlando, Fla.: Harcourt Brace Jovanovich, 1955.

Sledd, James. *A Short Introduction to English Grammar*. Glenview, Ill.: Scott, Foresman and Company, 1959.

Strunk, William, Jr., and E. B. White. *Elements of Style*. Third edition. New York: The Macmillan Co., 1979.

Zinsser, William K. *On Writing Well: An Informal Guide to Writing Nonfiction*. Second edition. New York: Harper & Row, Publishers, 1980.

Dictionaries

The American College Dictionary. New York: Random House, Inc., 1975.

American Heritage Dictionary of the English Language. Boston: Houghton-Mifflin Company, 1984.

Funk & Wagnalls Standard College Dictionary. New updated edition New York: T. Y. Crowell, 1977.

The Random House College Dictionary. Revised edition. New York: Random House, Inc., 1982.

The Random House Dictionary of the English Language. Unabridged edition. New York: Randon House, Inc., 1966.

Webster's Ninth New Collegiate Dictionary. Springfield, Mass.: Merriam-Webster, Inc., Publishers, 1983.

Webster's New World Dictionary. Second college edition. New York: Simon and Schuster, 1983.

Webster's Third New International Dictionary. Unabridged. Springfield, Mass.: Merriam-Webster, Inc., 1981.

Index

Numbers refer to the sections of this book.

Quick Reference Chart

		A	B	C	D
Grammar and Usage	**1**	Sentence parts 1-37	Parts of speech 38-52	Nouns 53-127	Pronoun classes 128-140
	2	Pronoun usage 141-169	Verbs 170-215	Verb usage 216-264	Verbals 265-274
	3	Adjectives 275-315	Adverbs 316-340	Prepositions 341-364	Conjunctions 365-386
Sentences	**4**	Sentence structure 387-416	Style and Variety 417-431	Effectiveness 432-436	Improving structure 437-463
Mechanics	**5**	Capitalization 464-485	Period, semicolon, colon 486-494	Comma 495-506	Quotation marks 507-516
	6	Apostrophe 517-521	Dash, parentheses, brackets 522-528	Question mark exclamation mark, hyphen 529-537	Abbreviations, italics, numerals 538-540
Organizing Ideas	**7**	Paragraph writing 541-550	Writing verse 564-576, 694	Planning and outlining 577-581	Business letters 587-615
	8	Social letters 616-624	Newspaper writing 625-632	Research paper 633-639	Oral communication 641-652
Diction	**9**	Classes of words 653-664	Usage Glossary 665-674	Figures of speech 676-682	Spelling and vocabulary 684-696

The letters at the top of the chart and the numbers at the left may be used as a simple code for composition correction. For example, C2 would refer to errors in verb usage.